# IMAGES OF BRADFORD
## 1860~1970

# IMAGES OF
# BRADFORD
## *1860~1970*

BB

BREEDON
BOOKS

First published in Great Britain by
The Breedon Books Publishing Company Limited
44 Friar Gate, Derby DE1 1DA
1992

ISBN 1 873626 05 3

Printed and bound in Great Britain by The Bath Press Ltd of Bath
and London.

# Contents

# Acknowledgements

The Publishers wish to extend thanks to Mrs Mabel Bruce, without whose photographs the Bradford Historical Survey Collection in the Central Library would be that much poorer; to Mrs Mary Stow for allowing the use of some of the late Mr N.Stow's photographs; The House of Fraser for access to the Brown, Muff & Co's photographic archives; and to Pratt's Furnishings, North Parade, for the use of some of Charles Pratt's superb pre-World War One photographs.

We are also indebted to the work of photographers Wade Hustwick, W.H.Wormersley ARPS, H.B.Priestley, N.S.Roberts ARPS, J.B.Scwires, H.Thackway, Morris E.Titterington ARPS, Miss Hind Smith, F.D.Smith and W.Hargreaves. Thanks are also due to the Trustees of the Imperial War Museum, the Bradford Heritage Recording Unit, Aerofilms Ltd and the Bradford *Telegraph and Argus.*

Special thanks go to the staff of the Bradford Reference Library, Tim Smith at the Bradford Heritage Recording Unit and John Triffitt of the Central Library.

# Introduction

THERE are always problems associated with compiling a book of this type. Should the book be an in-depth history with reams of facts and figures or a series of random dips into the past? Where should the book begin? And how should it end?

There are certainly facts and figures in this work but these tend to be in the form of additional snippets of information that are related, however distantly, to the topic of the photographs.

The book begins at St Peter's Church, which for nigh on three centuries dominated the Bradford skyline until overwhelmed by the ever-sprawling mass of chimney stacks and mill buildings. From St Peter's we begin what might be described as a 'photo safari' around the city centre, calling in at Forster Square, Market Street, Kirkgate, Ivegate, Hall Ings and so on, with a sequence of photographs dating from the late 1860s to 1973.

Some of the pictures are worth getting the magnifying glass on, as there is so much going on in them.

There is something fascinating about looking at photographs of days long gone, as one realises that the people in them experienced most of the same pleasures and trials that we feel are unique to us.

The second part of the book, looks at those townships and villages with strong, traditional ties with the city centre, such as Manningham, Bowling, Wyke, Low Moor, Wibsey, Little Horton, Great Horton, Thornton and Idle.

The exception to the rule is Queensbury. This book concerns itself with the period spanning broadly 1870-1970, but Queensbury was never a part of Bradford until the creation of the Metropolitan District Council in 1974. Other areas linked to Bradford in 1974, such as Baildon, Bingley, Bingley Rural, Denholme, Ilkley, Keighley, Shipley and Silsden are not included but will be dealt with later in a separate book.

In the second part of the book, the object of the exercise is to include buildings and areas long since gone, or altered beyond all recognition, as well as a look at everyday life, such as a wedding at Low Moor in 1900, a Whitsuntide singalong at Wyke, Black Dyke Mills, Queensbury and Idle from the air in 1925.

Several of Bradford's 'firsts' are also recorded here, including the first trolley bus, first Board school, first aerodrome, first fire-engine and first motor taxi-cab. Indeed, the city's pioneering spirit takes some beating, as the following list of 'firsts' shows:

1830 — The first Temperance Society in England was formed in Bradford.

1837 — The first Temperance Hall in England opened in Bradford.

1865 — Bradford was the first local authority to attempt to ban the building of back-to-back housing.

1872 — One of first local authorities to open a public library.

1872 — The Browne manual issuing system for library books was invented in Bradford.

1879 — One of first local authorities to commence slum clearances.

1889 — First local authority in the UK to build a generating station and commence electricity supplies to the public.

1891 — First independent Labour group formed in Bradford, the start of the National Independent Labour Party.

1891 — First authority in the UK to provide the wool industry with an independent testing laboratory.

1894 — First special classes held for 'feeble-minded' (special needs) children in England, at Whetley Lane School.

1899 — First school baths in the UK opened at Green Lane.

1899 — First school medical in the UK held at Usher Street School.

1900 — First local authority housing built in the UK was in Longland Street and Fairfax Street.

1907 — First school dinner provision in the UK.

1907 — First school milk provision in the UK.

1907 — Bradford became the first local authority in the UK to operate a railway (Nidd Valley Light Railway).

1908 — First sewage works in the UK to run at a profit, due to Esholt successfully extracting lanolin from waste and selling it to the cosmetics industry.

1908 — First school clinic in the UK.

1908 — First school breakfasts in the UK.

1911 — First trolley bus service in the UK. It was also the last, closing in 1972.

1914 — First camp school.

1914 — The 6th Battalion of the West Yorkshire Regiment was the first Territorial unit to report ready for action at the start of World War One.

1917 — First appointment by a local authority of municipal midwives.

1920 — One of the first nursery schools in the UK opened in Bradford.

But no matter how many firsts or lasts that Bradford can boast, by far the greatest impact has been visual with the redevelopment of the city centre in the 1960s. It is interesting to compare the pictures on page 22 to see what was there in 1923 and what had been replaced in 1965.

True, much needed bulldozing, but by the early 1970s some fine buildings had been lost forever including Swan Arcade, Kirkgate Market and the Mechanics Institute. We also seem to forget that the Victorians were quite happy to demolish Georgian, Jacobean and Elizabethan property, if it suited their purpose.

Hopefully this book will do justice to the photographs as they represent the efforts of many people, some alas unknown, who have cared enough about Bradford to go out in all weathers with their cameras.

The parish church of St Peter's prior to 1882, when the houses in front of the west door were demolished as part of a redevelopment scheme to make way for Forster Square, a new Post Office and a new station for the Midland Railway.

The parish church of St Peter's (it became a cathedral church in 1919) is thought to be the third place of worship to occupy the site. The discovery of two pieces of what is thought to be a Saxon preaching cross is the only evidence to support the theory that a church might have existed here from the late seventh century. What is known, however, is that a church built at some time around 1200 by the de Lacy family was destroyed by Scots raiders in 1327, during one of their frequent incursions into Yorkshire. The present building was begun in the mid-fourteenth century but work proceeded slowly and was not completed until 1458. The tower was a later addition, the work starting in 1493 and lasting 15 years. A clock was installed in the tower in 1666 and the thatched roof replaced with slate in 1724. In 1833 the interior underwent a major reconstruction; the song room and choir vestry were added in 1955 and a new east end was built in 1960.

*Opposite:* Looking north-west from the Bolling Chapel, 1957. *Mabel Bruce.*

This photograph shows the old chancel and east window. The window was installed in 1862 in memory of a local solicitor, Richard Tolson, and was built by William Morris to designs supplied by Dante Gabriel and Edward Burne-Jones. The window still exists, having been separated into three lights and installed in the Lady Chapel. Also in the picture is the font (right-hand foreground) and Colours of the West Yorkshire Regiment (The Prince of Wales's Own).

The enthronement of the Bishop of Bradford, the Rt Rev Ross Hook, 1972.

*Opposite:* City centre from the flats on Church Bank in June 1957. *W.Hargreaves (Bradford Photographic Society)*

*Above:* The Cathedral from Hall Ings in the early 1950s. On the left is H.Dawson & Sons and the Commercial Library. On the right is the HQ of the Bradford Dyers Association Ltd.

Photographed by Mr Macdonald, a city-bound tramcar rattles down Church Bank on 23 July 1949. The following day, motor buses took over on the Bradford Moor service, only to be superseded by trolley buses the following December.

A tram in trouble. The wreckage of tramcar No 210 lies outside the entrance to Sir Jacob Behrens & Sons, Well Street, on the 31 July 1907. The tram had been descending Church Bank towards Forster Square when the brakes failed due to a broken axle. The car ran out of control before shooting off the rails and coming to rest on its side with the top cover ripped off. That no one was killed was a minor miracle, although 14 people were injured.

Looking down Church Bank towards Forster Square *c.*1959. The trolley bus is only a few yards away from the scene of the July 1907 tram crash. The arched doorways led to Gillies Garnet & Co, Kilner & Co and Sir Jacob Behrens & Sons.

Forster Square one afternoon in 1891. The statue of W.E.Forster standing outside the Post Office was unveiled in 1890. At right foreground is the statue in memory of Richard Oastler (1789-1861) which was paid for by public subscription to honour the man who fought against the appalling working conditions and long working hours experienced by children in the local mills.

The year is 1897 and Forster Square is bedecked with flags and bunting for the celebrations marking Queen Victoria's Diamond Jublilee. That same year Bradford celebrated its 50th anniversary as a borough. The original Charter of Incorporation of 1847 had brought together the townships of Bradford, Manningham, Horton and Bowling, dividing them into eight wards. The council, having no purpose-built town hall at its disposal, held its meetings in Hall Ings Courthouse. By 1897, Bradford's ever-growing importance within the world's wool trade was acknowledged with the granting of city status.

Forster Square in the 1960s. The trams are now no more than a memory and within a few years the Square, too, would be redeveloped and be changed virtually beyond recognition.

Motor buses dominate Forster Square in this 1928 photograph by W.H.Womesley. The tramcar is on the Heaton service and is about to turn up Cheapside.

*Previous page:* Forster Square in 1931 looking towards the LMS station and Kirkgate. Tramcar No 11 is on the route 23 service — Undercliffe-Bingley via Forster Square and Saltaire. Part of the Bingley route — from Poplar House to Bingley Grammar School — was known as the 'golden mile' because the overhead wires were made of cadmium copper and did not turn green when exposed to the elements. The buildings on the right of the picture, containing the YMCA, were destroyed in a huge fire in 1950. *W.H.Womersley ARPS*

*Above:* Forster Square Station was 70 years old when this photograph was taken in June 1960. The Leeds & Bradford Railway opened on 1 July 1846, prior to which Brighouse had been the nearest railway station. Dixon's map of Bradford, prepared around 1846, showed a through railway line to the south from the L & BR but it was not until 1896 that the Midland Railway began to buy up property in central Bradford with a view to building such a line. The through-line scheme was approved by the Corporation in 1910 but abandoned by the Midland in 1919 as too costly. *Mabel Bruce*

View through the ornamental gates of Forster Square Station with the Post Office in the background.

The infamous Bradford Beck uncovered in September 1962. There was a time when the beck was little more than an open sewer into which household and mill waste alike was discharged. It was then used to top-up the water level in the canal basin which often resulted in a foul smelling toxic cocktail with occasionally flammable tendencies. Of the canal basin, James Smith, reporting on the condition of the town of Bradford in 1874, stated: 'In hot weather bubbles of sulphuretted hydrogen are continually rising to the surface, and so much is the atmosphere loaded with gas, that watch-cases and other materials of silver become black in the pockets of the workmen employed near the canal.' The beck also had a notorious reputation for flooding, especially during heavy storms. In 1768, a man and a boy were swept to their deaths by floodwater. There were floods in 1795 and again in 1822. In 1859 many buildings suffered from the combined effects of water and raw sewage. By 1866 the Corporation had had enough and took proceedings against the Canal Company in the High Court to restrain it from using the sewage-laden waters of the beck.

Looking toward Forster Square from Kirkgate in January 1971.

*Top:* The city centre in 1923 as photographed by N.S.Roberts from a height of 1,500ft (549 metres). Forster Square is in the centre foreground; *Bottom:* The city centre in early 1965. The new east end to the Cathedral is clearly visible and Forster Square is fast disappearing under several thousand tonnes of Portland Stone. It's hard to believe that in the 1850s the local quarries produced some of the finest stone available. *Aerofilms and Aero Pictorial Ltd.*

Forster Square in 1970.

*Above:* Looking toward Cheapside from Forster Square in January 1971. The 260-seat Cinecenta Twins cinema had opened in April 1969. It closed in September 1983.

The remodelled Cheapside, Market Street, Broadway end of Forster Square in July 1964. *Mabel Bruce.*

The Market Street junction with Forster Square as it was in the 1950s. Lingards was housed in what had previously been the Co-op, the latter having moved out in 1940. Lingards was demolished in 1959.

Looking down Market Street in 1959, just prior to the demolition of the former Lingards store which is at left foreground. On the right is the Boar's Head and Martins Cleaners, later a florist's shop.

Drivers of horse-drawn taxis await their next fares in Market Street *c.*1880. Until 1875, when the by-laws covering Hackney carriages were enforced, taxi drivers could charge what they liked. In 1871 there were 121 Hackney carriages licensed to operate in Bradford.

A Mabel Bruce picture of Market Street in September 1967. Compare this picture with the one on the previous page; whilst the buildings on the left-hand side are recognizable, the other side of the street has change beyond recognition.

Spinks Restaurant, Market Street, possibly in the 1870s.

The Anglo-South American Bank, Market Street. Note the shipping agency on the second floor. Manchester Liners, Prince Line and Houlder Line were all constituent companies of the Furness Witty group.

*Above:* One of Bradford's most famous retail stores had its origins in this draper's shop in Market Street, when Henry Brown inherited it from his mother. Brown took his brother-in-law, Mr Muff, into partnership to form Brown, Muff & Co. The business prospered and in 1870 the company moved into new premises on the corner of Ivegate and Market Street, their old shop being demolished as part of the redevelopment of the area. *House of Fraser.*

*Opposite top:* Delivery wagon of Brown, Muff & Co, in pre-internal combustion engine days. *House of Fraser.*
*Opposite (bottom):* Brown, Muff & Co's premises on the corner of Ivegate and Market Street. Over the years the company acquired the entire block, the last addition being a bank in 1934 which added 31,865 sq ft of floor space, giving a grand total of 103,200 sq ft. *House of Fraser.*

Brown, Muff & Co's toy department *c.*1933.

*Opposite  page  (top)*:  Boys'  schoolwear  department  at  Brown
Muff & Co.

*Opposite  page  (bottom):*  The  perfume  counter.

*Above:* Card department, possibly in January/February 1940.

*Right:* Brown, Muff & Co's ARP (Air Raid Precautions) crew. The man on the left is holding a scoop, of which there were many designs, used for removing incendiary bombs. *House of Fraser.*

*Left*: Exhibition of army life at Forster Square Station, sponsored by Brown, Muff & Co. *House of Fraser*.

*Below*: This photograph of a Brown, Muff & Co delivery van was probably taken around VE Day (Victory in Europe) in May 1945. Although the sign alludes to peace, the vehicle is still sporting its ARP headlight dimmers. Blackout restrictions were lifted on 23 April 1945. *House of Fraser*.

Market Street from the City Hall, c.1972.

*Above*: The junction of Leeds Road, Market Street and Bridge Street in 1959. The china store is holding a clearance sale due to the expiration of its lease, whilst smokers might have found a bargain or two at Walsh's, where a 'Compulsory Removal Sale' is underway. The Barclays Bank sign provides the tangible link between this picture and the one on the previous page. *Below:* The central area in 1925. Apart from one or two trams there is very little road traffic in evidence. *N.S.Roberts.*

Officials, workers and Post Office messenger boys pose with Matthew William, the Town Hall's big bell, which is about to be hauled into place in the 220ft-high (67 metres) campanile. Based on the campanile at the Palazzo Vecchio, Florence, the 13-bell carillon has a range of two octaves. Matthew William's job, then as now, is to strike the hours.

*Left* Three of the statues of 34 English monarchs and Oliver Cromwell which decorate the third-floor level of the City Hall. The most interesting statue is that of Richard III, who is thankfully not portrayed as the hunchback of Tudor propaganda.

*Below*: The first car in Bradford was this 3½HP Arnold Benz which was used by Joseph Dawson, a candidate for South Ward in the 1896 municipal election. It was also the year that the Light Locomotive Act removed restrictions on motorists; they could now drive at speeds in excess of 4 mph and no longer had to have a man walking in front waving a red flag; nor did they have to obtain a licence from each local authority whose district they wished to pass through. Bradford's first locally-built car also took to the roads in 1896. It was a 1½HP machine with a four-speed gearbox giving a maximum speed of 20mph.

The Town Hall was designed by Lockwood & Mawson, Bradford's leading architectural practice, in the mid-nineteenth century and famed for public buildings in Gothic or Italianate styles. Built of locally-quarried stone, construction began in 1870, the official opening taking place in September 1873. The building is essentially a neo-Gothic design but the clock tower is based upon that of the Palazzo Vecchio in Florence. This photograph dates from 1891 and in the distance is a rare view of the bottom of Leeds Road.

*Opposite Page:* The Town Hall in 1891. A horse-drawn omnibus can be seen coming out of Town Hall Street and there appears to be a queue of freight wagons developing at the corner of Nelson Street. On the Town Hall, the statues of English monarchs can be made out on the third floor. They were put there in 1873, prior to which they had been on public exhibition, although an admission charge was made on people wishing to view them. Two monarchs were, however, left out of the original scheme: Edward V, who held the throne for only a few weeks; and Queen Mary II, who ruled jointly with her husband, William of Orange.

Inside the Town Hall in 1891. *Above*: Magistrates' Court. *Below*: the Council Chamber.

*Above*: Alderman Godwin is proclaimed Bradford's first Lord Mayor, on Saturday, 5 October 1907, although Bradford had been granted city status in 1897
*Below*: Along from the Town Hall was Victoria Square.

*Above and right:*
Chapel Lane at the
side of the Town Hall
was the site of a Uni-
tarian chapel opened
in 1869 and photo-
graphed by Wade
Hustwick shortly
before its demolition
in 1969.

*Opposite page:* A
revised road scheme at
the junction of Nelson
Street and Norfolk
Street comes into oper-
ation in July 1967. The
City Hall looks superb
after cleaning.

*Opposite (top)*: Norfolk Street in 1938. On the left is the 1905 extension to the Town Hall, opened in 1909 and sympathetically designed by Norman Shaw to integrate with the original building. The tramcar is on a route 18 service to Tong Cemetery, whilst the double-deckers are Corporation-owned AEC and Leyland types *H.B.Priestley.*

*Below*: Town Hall Street in 1934. *W.H.Womersley ARPS.*

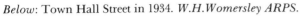

*Opposite page (bottom)*: Sunbridge Road, Westgate, Kirkgate and Kirkgate Market dominate this 1924 photograph by N.S.Roberts taken from an altitude of 1,700ft (518 metres).

*Above*: The Sunbridge Road-Bridge Street junction
with Market Street in April 1962.
*Right*: The headquarters of Bradford Corporation
Electricity Department, Sunbridge Road, June 1930.
Bradford was the first local authority in the UK to
build a generating station and commence supplies
to the public in 1889.

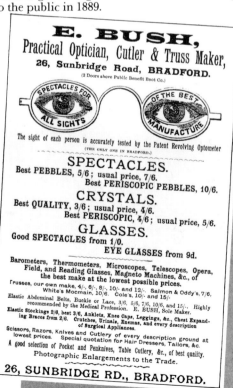

Window display of dining-room furniture at the Bradford Corporation Electricity Department showrooms, Sunbridge Road, in 1926.

Christmas display of 1930 at the BCED showrooms. The cardboard cut-outs of the children also appeared in the 1929 Christmas window. The one of the lady was a 'regular', featuring in a number of promotions from 1928 to about 1932.

FIRST BRADFORD GENERATING STATION
BOLTON ROAD   (360 H.P.)

OPENED 1889, CLOSED DOWN 1907.

★

"PRINCESS MARY" TURBO-GENERATOR
(40,000 H.P.) STARTED BY H.R.H. THE PRINCESS
MARY, COUNTESS OF HAREWOOD, IN 1930, AT
THE VALLEY ROAD POWER STATION

PRESENT CAPACITY OF PLANT, 140,000 H.P.

CITY OF                            BRADFORD
ELECTRICITY                        DEPARTMENT

HEAD OFFICES AND SHOWROOMS:
45 to 53 SUNBRIDGE ROAD, BRADFORD

*Where information regarding Use and Cost of Electricity for all
Purposes in the City can be obtained.*

THOMAS ROLES, M.I.E.E., *Engineer and Manager*

This advertisement from the souvenir booklet commemorating the 1931 Bradford Historical Pageant. It shows the recently-commissioned turbo-generator *Princess Mary*, installed at the Valley Road generating station. By the mid-1930s, Valley Road was the most powerful generating station under local authority control. In 1933 the highest peak load of electricity supplied in a single day was 59,400 kilowatts.

The Hotpoint Duplex vacuum cleaner is on sale at the BCED showrooms in May 1934, price £15 15s 0d (£15.75). The Hotpoint Junior is somewhat cheaper at £10 17s 6d (£10.88). However, in 1934 these were expensive items as few people earned more than three or four pounds per week.

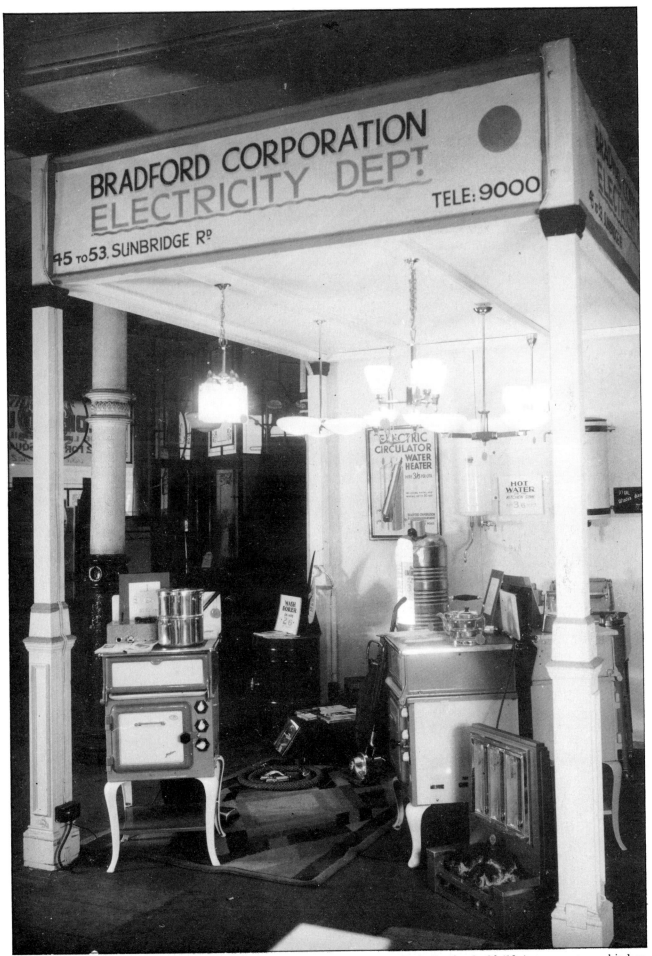

BCED stand at an exhibition in March 1936. It was possible to hire a wash boiler for 2s 6d (13p) per quarter, a kitchen sink water-heater for 3s 6d (18p) per quarter, or a 10-gallon water heater for 5s 0d (25p) per quarter.

Dating from May 1935, this truck toured the
streets extolling the virtues of electricity: 'At
a touch of the switch let electricity save you
labour, health and money.'

*Below*: Tyrrel Street looking towards
Sunbridge Road in September 1967. And
where better to go for a cup of tea after a
hard day's shopping than Collinson's Cafe.
The cafe was famous in the 1920s for its
tea dances.

*Left*: The New Inn at the corner of Tyrrel Street and Thornton Road was a local landmark for nearly 200 years before it was demolished in 1964. An important meeting place for textile manufacturers, dyers and merchants alike, a daily coach to Leeds and a weekly coach to Halifax stopped here, even though it was not officially a coaching inn. As well as being a hostelry, there was a time when the local Petty Sessions were held here and an old building standing round the back was known as the justices' room.

The Wool Exchange, like Kirkgate Market and the Town Hall, was designed by Lockwood & Mawson. Opened in 1867, it was from here that the world's wool industry would be influenced, if not controlled, for nearly 50 years until the export trade began to suffer from a combination of increased overseas production, foreign tariffs and currency restrictions. In 1924, unemployment among woollen trades workers stood at 7.3 per cent; by 1930 it was 26.1 per cent.

*Opposite Page*: Looking up Duckett Lane from Godwin Street. Duckett Lane ran parallel to Westgate, 1963.

*Right*: This photograph is of Bishop Blaize and is one of two adorning the Wool Exchange — the other is of King Edward III. Bishop Blaize is the patron saint of woolcombers due to his having been tortured to death by means of iron combs at Sebaste, Armenia, in AD316.

*Below*: The junction of Bank Street and Kirkgate in the late 1950s.

*Opposite page (top)*: Formerly the Crown & Cushion, the Old Crown, Ivegate, had, like its near-neighbour The Unicorn, a music or singing room which according to Bradford's Victorian moralists were veritable dens of iniquity. James Burnley of the *Bradford Observer* described the singing room of one pub as 'where songs, capable of an indecent interpretation, are freely indulged in'. The Old Crown was demolished in 1928.

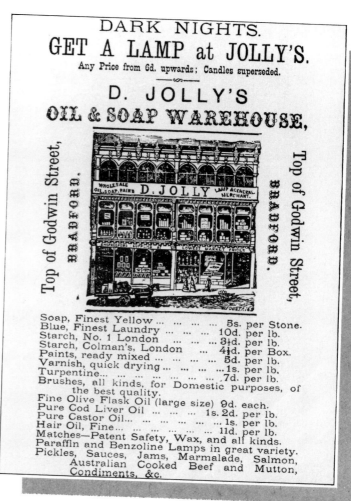

*Below*: Ivegate decorated for the Bradford Exhibition of 1904, held to celebrate the opening of the Cartwright Memorial Hall.

*Left*: Ivegate in the pre-World War One era. On the left is John Barraclough & Co (later a Yates Wine Lodge), whilst the Old Crown is on the right-hand side.

*Above:* Ivegate in 1960. The Old Crown, or rather Ye Olde Crown, is about halfway down on the right hand side and was built in 1928. *Mabel Bruce*

*Left:* The junction of Ivegate and Kirkgate, *c.*1885.

*Above*: The old Manor Hall and its surrounds had seen better days when this photograph was taken shortly before its demolition. Built by William Rawson, Lord of the Manor, in 1705, to replace Bradford Hall, it remained the Rawson family seat for over a century before being let to John Hardy, who was an MP for Bradford from 1832-1837 and again from 1841-1847. The Hardys moved out in 1825 and the grounds and gardens were used for a market, the Hall itself eventually becoming Goodchild's Temperance Hotel. In 1866, the Council paid the Rawsons £5,000 for a 999-year lease on the market rights and 18,000 sq yds of land. The Hall was demolished and Kirkgate Market built to the design of Lockwood & Mawson.

*Below*: Kirkgate in 1877 with Kirkgate Market in the distance. The building at right foreground is the banking house of Beckett & Co, a firm originally established in 1803 by Edmund Peckover and his nephew, Charles Harris, as Peckover, Harris & Co. The firm survived in various guises, J.H.& A.Harris & Co., then the Bradford Old Bank, to go public in 1864 and be eventually absorbed into Barclays. A bank was established in Bradford in 1760 but collapsed 21 years later. The town's first savings bank, the East Morley & Bradford, opened in 1818; by 1856 its opening hours were 2.30pm to 4.30pm on Thursdays and Saturdays, and Saturday evenings 6pm until 8pm. Competition for the East Morley & Bradford arrived in 1861 with the opening of a branch of the Post Office Savings Bank. However, on a number of occasions Bradford investors got their fingers burnt, the most noteable being the collapse of Wentworth, Rishworth & Chaloner in 1825, the Land Mortgage Bank of Florida in 1896, which incidentally had its HQ in Bradford, and the Charing Cross Bank in 1910.

*Above*: Sales drive at Montague Burton's shop, Kirkgate, for Laird Scottish tweed suits at just 55s 0d (£2.75).

*Right*: Craven's Tea Rooms, otherwise stall No.1 in Kirkgate Market. Here, Mr Craven is assisted by Miss Boxshall.

*Opposite page*: Work on Kirkgate Market began in 1871 but was not completed until 1878. Designed by Lockwood & Mawson, this grand building survived until the early 1970s when it fell victim to a plan to demolish it. When the plan was exposed in *Private Eye* the repercussions reverberated around the city and led to the eventual bankruptcy of John Poulson. *Mabel Bruce*.

The interior of Kirkgate Market in 1972, showing part of the ornate ironwork. For years, the market operated at a profit but little was spent on essential maintenance.

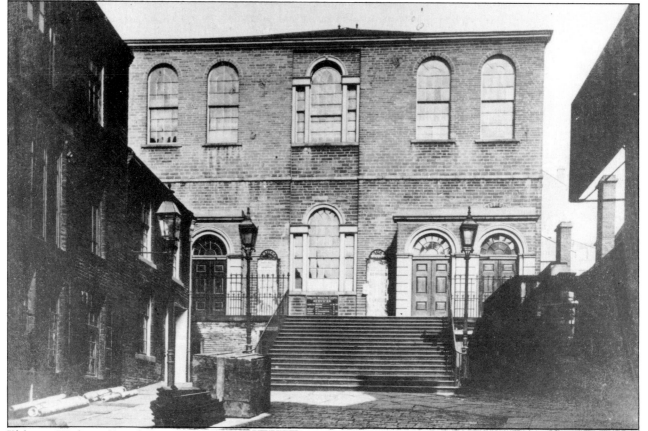

Kirkgate Weslyan Chapel, opened in 1811 replacing the Octagon, the earliest local purpose-built Weslyan Chapel, in Great Horton Road.

Chapel Court, off Kirkgate, photographed by Mabel Bruce in June 1964.

*Left*: Entrance to Dunn's Arcade, June 1964.

*Opposite page*: Laycock's Yard to Dunns Arcade in June 1964; note entrance to public air-raid shelter on left. *Mabel Bruce.*

*Top*: The Jolly Butchers in Rawson Place sold Bass beer, Guiness stout, Bentley's Yorkshire ales, cider and Bovril. The posters are of particular interest, advertising a Rugby League game between Bradford and Salford and two Bradford Cup semi-final clashes: Bradford City v Girlington and Airedale v Cullingworth. The photograph dates from about 1902.

*Left*: James Gate off James Street led through to Westgate. The Tetley's pub is the Boy and Barrel, formerly owned by Melbourne Ales, 1963 *Mabel Bruce.*

Morrison's first self-service store was in James Street. *Bradford Heritage Recording Unit.*

Bradford's second retail market, in Rawson Place, was started in 1871 and opened in 1875 for the sale of meat, fish, vegetables and fruit.

Interior of Rawson Place pictured in the 1970s.

Northgate looking towards North Parade, July 1967. *Mabel Bruce.*

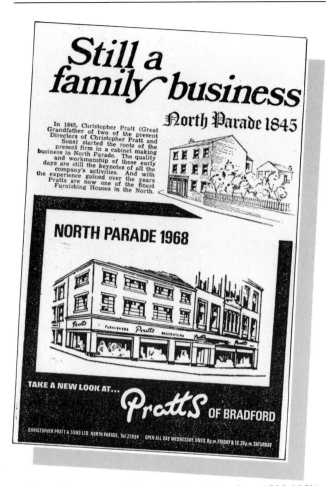

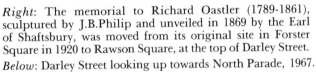

*Right*: The memorial to Richard Oastler (1789-1861), sculptured by J.B.Philip and unveiled in 1869 by the Earl of Shaftsbury, was moved from its original site in Forster Square in 1920 to Rawson Square, at the top of Darley Street.

*Below*: Darley Street looking up towards North Parade, 1967.

The Midland Bank at the junction of Darley Street and Kirkgate in August 1964. *Mabel Bruce.*

*Below*: The former head office of the Leeds & Liverpool Canal Company, Manor Row. The Canal Company was formed in 1770, the first section (Skipton-Bingley) opening for traffic in 1773. Bradford, not being on the original route, was linked to the main canal by a three-mile branch which ran north from a basin near Broadstones to Windhill and opened in 1774. There were problems: the canal basin was topped up with the polluted waters of Bradford Beck, things getting so bad that in 1866 a High Court injunction was obtained forbidding the Canal Company from using the beck. The canal was closed but a new Bradford Canal Company opened for business in 1871, a new terminus and warehouses having been built near the Zetland Mill. The old basin and about 400 yards of canal were sold off for building. The most important feature of the new company was the commissioning of a series of pumping stations to bring water from the Leeds & Liverpool Canal to the new basin. Traffic, however, was light and the branch closed for good in 1922.

*Opposite (top)*: The Salem Congregational Church was established in Bradford in 1836 and this photograph shows part of the burial ground at their chapel in Manor Row. In 1908 the chapel was converted into the first school clinic in the country. This photograph was taken shortly before the site was turned into a car park. *Wade Hustwick.*

*Opposite (bottom)*: The Registry Office, Manor Row, was opened in 1877 as the Poor Law Building, where the Board of Govenors administered the provisions of the Poor Law Act to the destitute.

Warehouse and office block in Cheapside, January 1960.

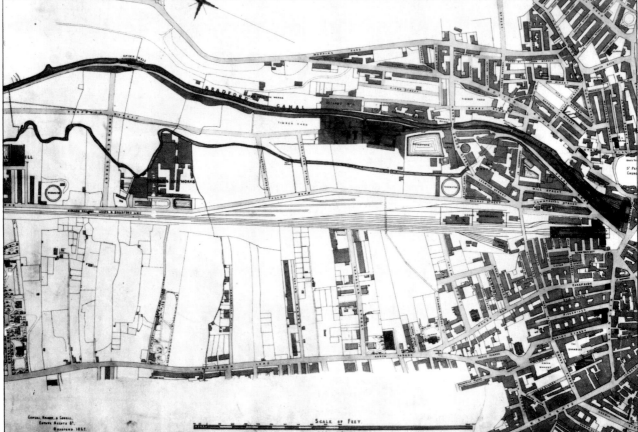

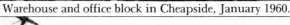

Plan of the Bradford Canal prepared in 1867 by estate agents Cowgill, Knight & Cowgill.

*Previous page*: Bermondsey, at the bottom of Kirkgate, pictured before 1885. The Midland Railway hoarding entreats the citizens of Bradford to emigrate to New Zealand, Australia or the Cape. Passage to Australia cost £5 third-class, £15 second-class, details available on request from J.Barron, Government Agent, Westgate.

General view of the Canal Road-Bolton Road area of the city in 1923. The photograph was taken at an altitude of 3,000 ft (915 metres) by N.S.Roberts.

*Below*: View across the city centre in March 1965 as Gothic, Georgian and Italianate architecture gives way to high-rise blocks.

The junction of Booth Street and Broadway was already scheduled for demolition when this photograph was taken in March 1959.

June 1960. Construction continues apace on the Market Street, Broadway and Broadway Forster Square blocks. *Mabel Bruce.*

*Left*: The new C&A store, Broadway, 1959. *C.H.Wood.*

Broadway Precinct was opened in April 1971. In the background is Britannia House and the ABC Cinema. The ABC organization was the creation of Glasgow lawyer, John Maxwell, and by 1937 they had 431 cinemas compared to Gaumont-British's 345 and Odean's 300, out of a nationwide total of 4,734.

*Above*: Lonian Textiles, Topham's Typewriters and Central Burling Company would soon be moving out as demolition was imminent. The block was bounded by Swaine Street, Charles Street and Hall Ings. August 1959.

*Below*: Another block due for demolition in August 1959, perhaps the one bounded by Swaine Street, Colliergate, Hall Ings and Booth Street.

The end is nigh for the old H.Dawson & Sons building, Hall Ings. Visible in this picture is the south wing which was added to the Cathedral in the 1950s to provide facilities for Cathedral staff.

Milligan & Forbes warehouse, Hall Ings.

*Above*: Hall Ings, Drake Street and Leeds Road, October 1963.

*Below*: The new-look Hall Ings in September 1967. The view is in the direction of Leeds Road and the junction with Petersgate.

*Top (left)*: Bridge Street from Sunbridge Road in 1968. The Mechanics Institute is on the right-hand side of the picture, just beyond Saxones Shoes.

*Left (middle)*: The Mechanics Institute was formed in February 1832 and early meetings were held in a room above a shop in Kirkgate, but in 1840 premises were obtained in Leeds Road. The foundation stone of the Bridge Street building was laid on 28 January 1870, the official opening being performed by W.E.Forster in 1873. The Institute was at the forefront of the campaign to keep Bradford's textile industry at the top. Weaving and design classes were started in 1877 and technical classes, sponsored jointly with the Chamber of Commerce, began in 1878. The Technical School became independent of the Institute in 1882, when the Prince and Princess of Wales opened a new college in Great Horton Road. Shown is the concert hall as it was in 1972.

*Below*: The library at the Mechanics Institute, 1972. On 4 July 1973 there was a public demonstration against the demolition of this fine building.

The Bowling Green Hotel, Bridge Street, was built in 1750 on the site of a sixteenth-century inn, but was itself demolished in the 1860s to make way for the Mechanics Institute. There was a bowling green behind the hotel.

*Above*: St George's Hall was Bradford's first important civic building of the Victorian era. The foundation stone was laid in 1851 with full Masonic honours and the opening celebrations in 1853 were marked with a three-day music festival. Designed by Lockwood & Mawson and built of Leeds Stone, the Hall's neo-classical lines were a distinctive feature of the town's skyline. That St George's Hall was built in the first place was due to the Corporation being lobbied by influential members of the town's music fraternity for the provision of a public assembly hall. The earliest record of any musical event taking place in Bradford is of a performance of *Messiah* staged in the Piece Hall in 1774. Twelve years later an oratorio was performed at St Peter's Church to celebrate the installation of its first organ. Bradford Musical Friendly Society was formed in 1821.

*Right*: St George's Hall organ as rebuilt in 1953 and *opposite page (top)* the Bradford choir.

The brick structure in the foreground of this November 1971 picture is the new Queen's pub, whilst across the road stands the Victoria Hotel. The 1927 edition of *Baedecker's Great Britain* lists the hotel as the Great Northern Victoria with 60 bedrooms at prices from 7s 6d (38p) per night. Breakfast and lunch were available at 4s 0d (20p), dinner was somewhat expensive at 6s 6d (33p).

The splendid interior during a concert at St George's Hall in the 1950s.

*Below*: The skeletal remains of Bradford Exchange Station. Opened in 1867, Exchange Station replaced an earlier one at Adolphus Street. In the 1880s, congestion often meant that trains ran late out of Exchange Station. In February 1881, woolbuyers who had intended to travel on the 3.10pm to London, were so incensed by the late running of their train that they demanded a refund and caught the 3.45pm Midland Railway train instead. Lack of a turntable meant the engine and carriages had had to turn on the St Dunstan's triangle and, although they left early enough, they became caught up in the chaos of trains outside the station.

The bottom of Wakefield Road at the junction of Bridge Street in 1960.

*Top (right)*: 'Time ladies and gentlemen please!' was soon to have a permanent ring about it for the regulars of the Queen Hotel, Bridge Street. The building dated back to 1775 but had been owned by Hammonds since 1914. The pub, once the popular haunt of railwaymen, was demolished in the 1960s. *Mabel Bruce.*

*Middle (right)*: One of Bradford's smallest but by no means unimportant edifices was the 'Gents' near the Queen Hotel, Bridge Street. It was demolished in December 1968, forcing its patrons to seek relief elsewhere.

*Below*: Union Street, March 1961. In the distance is Stockton Wools Ltd and J.Ormondroyd & Co, Nelson Street. Buses could be caught here for Holme Wood, West Bowling and New Cross Street. *Mabel Bruce.*

In the 1840s, Union Street linked Bridge Street with Nelson Street and the back-to-back housing of such places as Fawcett Court, Fawcett Row, Hope Street, King Street and Clarence Street. Going down Union Street from Bridge Street, the left-hand side was dominated by Walker's Mill, the right-hand side being comprised of business premises which gave way to a number of back courts, the nearer one got to the junction with Nelson Street. This photograph dates from 1932. On the left is the Prince's Restaurant and on the right is Bailey & Wall.

*Left:* In 1934, the London Fire Brigade took delivery of the first Dennis limousine-type fire appliance to be built and other brigades were quick to follow. This Bradford appliance was also built by Dennis in 1934, although Leyland and Merryweather were building similar machines by 1935.

*Opposite page (top):* Central Fire Station, Nelson Street, c.1955. Nearest the camera is KY7117, the 1934 Dennis limousine-type tender in its rebuilt form. The next three machines appear to be Dennis F12 dual-purpose appliances powered by Rolls-Royce B80MKX petrol engines capable of accelerating from 0-60mph (0-97kph) in 45 seconds and fitted with the MK3 pump which delivered 900gpm. Beyond the F12s are a pair of turntable-ladder machines. The fire station was built in 1901-02.

*Opposite page (bottom):* The Odeon Cinema, Manchester Road. Odeon Cinemas was founded in 1933 by Oscar Deutsch with the support of United Artists and was the largest builder of super-cinemas in the mid-1930s, each new theatre being opened amidst a blaze of publicity. Bradford's 2,685-seater Odeon opened on 17 December 1937, the ceremony being performed by the Lord Mayor, Alderman T.J.Robinson, and also by Clive Brook, star of the opening film, *The Ware Case* which was being world-premiered. Brook spoke of Bradford's Odeon as 'this beautiful theatre', which was true as all of the group's cinemas were ultra-modern and made much use of opaque glass and chromium.

*Right*: The Odeon's auditorium. In the 1930s cinema takings in the UK amounted to £40 million a year with ticket sales running at 20 million a week, which meant that 40 per cent of the population went to the pictures more than once a week. Cinema building continued throughout the 1930s. In 1935 there were 4,448 cinemas in the UK, by 1937 there were 4,734 and by 1938 there were 4,967. Bradford's Odeon closed on Saturday 22 March 1969, the name being transferred to the Gaumont, Prince's Way. *J.B.Scwires.*

*Below*: Looking down Portland Street from Manchester Road on a lazy sunny afternoon in June 1960, towards Bedford Street. Sandwiched between Portland Street and Clifford Road were Marshall's Mill and the Britannia Mill. Britannia Street cuts across this picture at right angles. *H.Thackway.*

City of Bradford Co-operative Society branch No.1 in Manchester Road. The first Co-operative Society in the area was formed at Queensbury in 1855. The City of Bradford Co-op was formed in 1901 by the amalgamation of the Bradford Provident Industrial Society and the West Bowling Co-operative Society and by 1910 had 20,000 members and capital of £427,000. The Bradford Provident had been formed in 1860 and in its first year made a profit of £33 from its shop in Bridge Street. Also formed in 1860 was the Bradford Industrial, their retail outlet being in Queensgate. In 1868, the Bradford Provident and Bradford Industrial amalgamated under the Provident's name. The movement prospered and in 1903 the first Co-op laundry in the country was opened in Bradford. Further amalgamations took place, including the Eccleshill Industrial Society in 1925, Allerton Industrial Co-operative Society in 1931 and Birkenshaw Industrial Society in 1933.

Adelaide Street, between Clifford Street and Duncan
Street, was the home of small businesses dealing in
wool noils and waste, such as J.Naylor & Co,
Wadsworth & Son, James M.Walker Ltd and Stanley
Walker & Son. At the bottom of the street is the Waterloo
Mill. *Wade Hustwick.*

These shops at the junction of Franklin Street and Manchester Road are a typical example of the types of retail business to be found outside any city centre in the country and providing a valuable service to the people living in nearby streets. *Morris E.Titterington.*

The Craven Heifer, Smiddles Lane in 1960. The new pub built to replace it can just be seen on the left of the photograph.

*Previous four pages*: Road widening underway at Manchester Road, Truncliffe, in the 1920s, with the tramlines clearly seen on the cobbled surface and debris being collected by horse and cart.

*Above*: The old rate office at the junction of Holroyd Hill and Wibsey Bank, Wibsey, *c*.1900.

*Left*: The Windmill Inn, High Street, Wibsey, when trolley buses still plied the route from Bradford. It was just before World War One that routes were given numbers and the Wibsey via Morley Street, Laisterbridge Lane and Little Horton service became route No.1, the reason being that Alderman Priestley's ward was Wibsey and he was chairman of the Tramways Board.

The Horse and Groom Inn, Wibsey, when the landlord, Gent Ormondroyd kept order. Note the extension to the building, clearly visible in this picture dating from around 1900.

The centre-piece of Wibsey Park's flower beds in 1928 was this floral organ. The decoration was changed every year, in 1930 it was an ambitious affair, three walls of a parlour room, fireplace, two easy chairs and a couple of paintings.

*Above:* Halifax Road, Buttershaw, *c.*1916. Tomlinson's corner shop and off-licence was at the junction with Fleece Street, the Bee-Hive Inn just across the road was flanked by Bee-Hive Yard and Bee-Hive Street. The local mill and mill ponds were opposite the inn but set back off the main road.

*Opposite Page (top):* Odsal Stadium opened in 1934, the original stand being the one on the left in our picture. The home of Bradford Northern RLFC, the ground had an estimated capacity for 200,000 spectators and in 1954, 102,569 fans watched the Challenge Cup Final replay between Halifax and Warrington. The highest attendance for a Bradford Northern game was 64,429, for a match against Huddersfield in March 1953. The photograph dates from the mid-1960s, when both club and ground had experienced hard times. The club had folded mid-way through the 1963-4 season but had recently reformed. The ground had received some attention with part of the terracing being re-laid. *Aerofilms Ltd.*

*Opposite page (bottom):* The Victoria Hotel, Huddersfield Road, *c.*1902. There is a story that in the days when a certain Squire Hodgson kept the Victoria, he made a point on pay-night of asking the men if they'd been home first. If they had, then fine, they could drink themselves silly if they wished; if not, the Squire would allow them only a drop and then send them home. For years the Vic was known locally as 'The Drop'.

Low Moor Cottage Baths at the corner of North Street and School Street, opened on 18 July 1904. The baths were converted from a cottage and a shop at a cost of £412. A popular place at weekends, there were three slipper-baths for ladies, three for men and one slipper-bath and two table-baths for children.

*Right:* 'Marriage: The marriage took place on Tuesday at Holy Trinity Church, Low Moor, of Mr William Henry Rayner and Miss Susannah Hustler.'

The father of the bride, William Henry Rayner, standing proudly outside his shop. 'The ceremony, which was conducted by the Rev. J.W. Naylor, curate, was one which attracted a large congregation, both the contracting parties being well known. The bride wore a dress of mohair-figured lustre, trimmed with ivory Duchesse satin, pearls and silk chiffon, and her attendant maids were in cream. After the ceremony the party drove around Hartshead and Brighouse and in the afternoon about 160 guests sat down to tea provided in the Weslyan Reform schoolroom by Mrs Bailey. The presents, which were numerous and valuable, included a tea-service from the teachers of the Sunday school and a gold chain given by the bridegroom to the bride. *Cleckheaton Guardian, 1 June 1900.*

Haley's shoe shop, School Street. Just what were Woodmilne 'revolving heels'?

The refinery at Low Moor, *c.*1906.

The plate mill opened in 1867.

*Opposite page (top)*: Low Moor, *c.*1906. The township was dominated by the iron works, which in 1863 employed 3,600 workers producing best Yorkshire iron for customers world wide. By 1928 the company was in serious financial difficulties, partially self-inflicted due to its inability to adapt, and partially due to the onset of a recession, resulting in closure and the loss of 3,000 jobs.

*Opposite (bottom)*: Eight-ton steam hammer installed at Low Moor in 1864. A four-ton hammer had been installed some 20 years earlier and this was used in 1857 to forge parts for Isambard Kingdom Brunel's paddle steamer *The Great Eastern*.

*Right*: Blast furnace, *c.*1906. The first blast furnaces at Low Moor were commissioned in 1791 and by 1850 had produced enough slag to bury the Pyramids. The oldest blast process in the area, by means of a cold-air blowing engine, had been installed at Birkenshaw Foundry in 1782, prior to which the process had been dependent upon weather conditions as cold air at very low pressure had to be used, resulting in better quality iron being produced in winter.

*Below*: View of the newly-erected blast furnaces, *c.*1905. But the demand for wrought iron was about to go into decline as cheaper steels were readily available. Another problem facing Low Moor was that local mineral resources were nearly exhausted. Wrought-iron, no matter how versatile or corrosion resistant, was an expensive commodity to produce and the prospect of having to import essential raw materials from outside the local area could only add to the cost of finished products.

One of the 3ft gauge locomotives used on the Low Moor Ironworks Railway.

Bradford's first motor-driven fire-engine and the brigade's last pair of horses pose for the camera in 1914. On the left, Fireman Tom Farrar holds on to Captain, whilst on the right, Fireman Knighton Pridmore looks after Nelson. The driver of the fire-engine is Tom Cousens who drove the engine from the makers back to Bradford. Cousens joined the brigade reluctantly as a driver-mechanic in 1908 — he was the only one who could drive — on the understanding that he was a driver, not a fireman. However, Tom often joined in with the firefighting without being asked. Sitting next to him is Fireman Jim Evett. On 21 August 1916, his engine was destroyed in the Low Moor Munitions Works disaster, Fireman Knighton Pridmore being one of those killed. Tom Farrar modelled for the memorial which was later erected in Scholemoor Cemetery.

On 21 August 1916, an explosion occurred at the New Works Road site of the Low Moor Chemical Company, where pitric acid was being manufactured for the munitions industry. The local works brigade, unable to contain the subsequent fires, called for help from Bradford Fire Brigade. About half an hour after their arrival, the regular firemen were either dead or in hospital, having been caught in a second explosion. At the nearby North Bierley Works, a gasometer holding around 270,000 cubic feet of gas was hit by falling debris, ruptured and then blew up causing extensive damage to housing and rolling stock in the nearby carriage sidings.

Tramcar No.192 at Wyke, *c*.1905. The building is Wyke Board School, a product of the W.E.Forster-inspired Education Act of 1870. At that time, religious, factory and private schools in the town were providing places for 19,000 children out of an estimated 80,000. By 1874, eight Board Schools were up and running, the first being Bowling Back Lane, another 13 opening by 1885.

Pupils and teacher at Wyke Board Girls School, 1931.

Huddersfield Road, Wyke, *c*.1912. The photograph is thought to show work on the tramway extension from Wyke to Bailiff Bridge, where Halifax Corporation Tramways had a terminus. From March 1913 it was possible to travel from Bradford to Huddersfield by tram, changing at Bailiff Bridge and at Brighouse. In June 1944, the Bradford-Wyke and Bailiff Bridge services were converted to motor buses.

A Whitsuntide singalong at Town Gate, Wyke. The photograph is dated 1950s but looks more like the late 1930s.

Wyke Champion Brass Band in the Plantation House Gardens, Whitehall Road in 1923. *Miss Hind Smith.*

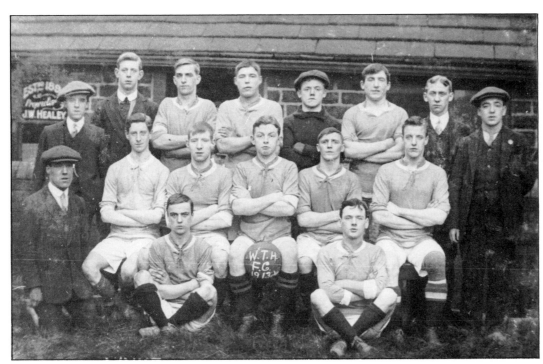

One of the many temperance movement football teams was Wyke Temperance Hall AFC, seen here at the start of the 1913-14 season. The first temperance society in England had been formed in Bradford in 1830 and the first temperance hall in the country (later Jowett Hall) opened in 1837.

This photograph dating from around 1935 shows the Wyke Old Boys FC side being presented to Lord Harewood before the kick-off in a game against Leeds United.

Wyke Home Guard unit on 12 July 1941. It was on 14 May 1940 that the Secretary of State for War, Sir Anthony Eden, broadcast an appeal for men aged 17 to 65 to form a new force whose prime function would be to guard factories, railways, canals and other vital installations and to oppose enemy paratroopers until regular troops could join the battle. Within minutes of Eden's broadcast, men were arriving at police stations to enrol. Initially the new force was designated the Local Defence Volunteers. In August 1944, the War Office announced that the force would be stood down on 3 December.

This crossing with watchman's cabin was one of six in the Low Moor and Wyke area on the mineral lines of the Low Moor Co. When the watchmen and cabins were eventually done away with, it became the job of the fireman to get off the locomotive and stop any road traffic. This particular photograph is of the level crossing in Wilson Road, Wyke.

*Above*: Salt Horn, Oakenshaw, *c*.1907. The railway station can be seen in the background and it was from here that the Midland Railway proposed to build a link to Forster Square by means of a tunnel over two miles long under Bierley Top and Bowling Park, thus giving Bradford a through route. The scheme was abandoned in 1906 for both practical and financial reasons.

*Left*: 'Where to find us' postcard issued by Thomas Wright (Bradford) Ltd. Of interest, although not labelled, are the Bus Station, the Cenotaph and part of the Gaumont.

The Cenotaph at the bottom of Little Horton Lane was unveiled in 1922. The previous year the Roll of Honour of local men who had served in World War One was completed, containing 36,625 names including the 5,243 who were killed outright or subsequently died of wounds. *Mabel Bruce.*

Excellent study of the auditorium of the Prince's Theatre. *N.Stow, courtesy of Mrs Mary Stow.*

In the mid-1870s, Bradford had the Victorian equivalent of a performing arts complex. Built on the site of the old St John's Church at the bottom of Little Horton Lane, the basement, better known as the Star Music Hall, opened in August 1875. The upper part, the Prince's Theatre, where the serious stuff was staged, opened its doors on 17 April 1876 with the Carl Rosa Opera Company doing the honours. The Prince's certainly had a colourful existence. Burned down in July 1878, it was rebuilt and used as an accommodation block by the Salvation Army until the purpose-built barracks was opened in Sefton Street.

Reverting to theatrical use, the Prince's was taken over by Pullan's (owners of Pullan's Music Hall near John Street Market) before passing into the hands of the irrepressible Francis Laidler. He did his upmost to turn the Prince's into one of the leading provincial theatres, bringing in top performers and major productions from London. From the early 1930s until its eventual closure, the Prince's was mainly used as a repertory theatre. This building, so full of character, was demolished in 1964, yet another sacrifice on the altar of modernization. *N.Stow, courtesy of Mrs Mary Stow.*

*Left*: The stage at the Prince's. In the good old days, the stages of the Prince's and the Music Hall were back-to-back and it is said that on more than one occasion an artist found himself on the wrong stage. *N Stow, courtesy of Mrs Mary Stow.*

The Fox and Pheasant Inn, Little Horton, c.1900.

The old West Yorkshire Bus Station was a useful short-cut between Little Horton Lane and Great Horton Road. The photograph dates from March 1966 and the Silver Blade Ice Rink can be seen in the background. *Mabel Bruce.*

Carnival time in Little Horton, 1907.

*Above*: The former Baptist College in Park Road when in use as a children's home. The Baptists had been in Horton since 1655 and a preaching house at Heaton existed in the 1690s but closed down after a few years, only to be re-established by 1711. The Horton Baptist College was established in 1804 by the Northern Education Society in an old weaving shed, later moving to grander premises. In 1859 the college closed, students and staff transferring to a similar institution at Rawdon.

*Opposite page (top)*: The home of Bradford Park Avenue FC in 1965. The ground was opened in 1880, when Park Avenue played rugby, but in 1907 they changed to soccer and in 1914 reached the heady heights of the First Division, where they remained until 1921. From then on, despite having some outstanding individual players, Park Avenue were on the downhill slope. In 1970 they failed to gain re-election to the Football League and eventually folded in 1974. Since this photograph was taken, not only is the original football club just a memory, the railway lines have gone too, the line to Queensbury having been long dismantled. *Aerofilms Ltd.*

Bradford Schools' Sports Association meeting at Park Avenue, 1968.

Competitors and spectators at the 1968 meeting of the Bradford Schools' Sports Association.

*Right*: Batons at the ready during the 1968 Bradford Schools' Sports Association meeting at Park Avenue.

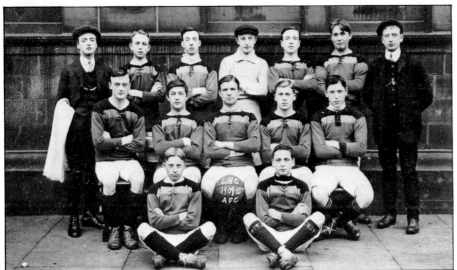

*Left (top)*: Park Avenue, the scene of many a clash in the Yorkshire Schools Cup. Bradford Boys side for the 1932-3 season. The players are un-named but the teachers are (left to right): Mr Coogan (St Bedes), E.Richmond (Low Moor), Jack Hodgson (Thorpe), J.S.Nicholson (Whetley Lane), Arthur Randall (Ryan Street), H.Cooper (St Augustine's) Mr.Dawson (St Michaels), Sam Firth (Low Moor), Wilf Morley (Drummond), Mr Bokes (Wellington Road), A.J.Evans (Woodroyd), Arthur Spencer (Bowling Back Lane), A.Holriyd (Princeville) and W.Padget (Priestman).

*Left (middle)*: Little Horton AFC, 1909-10 season, taken at Southfield Lane.

*Below*: Horton Park, pre-World War One.

The year is 1908 and tramcar No.138 clatters along St Enoch's Road towards Wibsey. The road was named after Alderman Enoch Priestley, who had instigated the building of the road and the tramway to Wibberley.

Rand's Mill once occupied the site where the Alhambra now stands. The mill was demolished to make way for street improvements but when the project was completed, some 1,500 square yards of land remained derelict. In 1897, the Corporation sold it for about £8,000 to William Greenwood, but it remained undeveloped until leased by Francis Laidler.

# ALHAMBRA THEATRE, BRADFORD

*Magnificent Attraction*
*for the week of the*
**BRADFORD HISTORICAL PAGEANT**
Commencing Monday, July 13th, 1931.   TWICE NIGHTLY, 6-30 & 8-40

FRANCIS LAIDLER'S GRAND NEW REVUE

## "SAY IT WITH LAUGHTER"

A BRILLIANT PRODUCTION

A BRITISH SHOW *played by* BRITISH ARTISTES *presented by*
A BRITISH PRODUCER

CAST INCLUDES

### GWLADYS STANLEY

GEORGE, FRED *and* BERT SANGER          MARY *and* JANE
EVIE CARCROFT          STEPHANIE ANDERSON'S MID-AIR GIRLS
A ROLLS ROYCE CHORUS          SCENES OF SPLENDOUR

### HAL BRYAN

LIVING ARTISTES—LIVING BEAUTY—LIVING COMEDY—LIVING SPECTACLE

**The Show of the Year**

GWLADYS STANLEY

PRICES OF ADMISSION (including Tax)
MONDAY to FRIDAY:  6d., 1/2, 1/6, 2/4          SATURDAY:  9d., 1/6, 2/-, 3/-
ALL SEATS BOOKABLE IN ADVANCE WITHOUT EXTRA CHARGE
BOX OFFICE  9-30 a.m. to 8-0 p.m.          TELEPHONE 5679

Remembrance Day, November 1967. The back-drop is provided by the Alhambra Theatre and the Gaumont Cinema. The Gaumont, when opened in 1930 as the New Victoria, had 3,318 seats and was the largest cinema in the provinces (the Gaumont State, Kilburn, had 4,000 seats, the Hammersmith Gaumont 3,387 and the Davis Theatre, Croydon, 3,725). The name was changed to the Gaumont in 1950 and in 1968 it was closed for conversion into a bingo hall (seating for 2,000) and twin cinema (467 seats and 1,207 seats).

W.I.Blakeley's shop in Horton Road. The photograph was taken during the run-up to a Christmas, date unknown, as that was the only time Blakeleys stocked satsumas. Mr and Mrs Blakeley, along with young Master Blakeley, stand in the entrance.

The Alexandra Hotel, Great Horton Road, was designed by Andrews & Pepper and opened in 1879. The unusual feature was the addition some 20 years later of a music hall, the Empire, which was built on to the back. The Empire was converted into a 1,381-seater cinema during World War One, re-opening under New Bio-Colour Circuit management on 11 February 1918, passing into Gaumont British ownership in 1937. In January 1952 the cinema was badly damaged by fire and never re-opened.

*Left*: The Moorish Tearooms and Miss Gabrielle Hope and the All-ladies Orchestra were but a memory in September 1962, when this photograph of the tattered remains of the Empire Theatre was taken.

*Below*: The bottom of Great Horton Road looking towards the Alexandra Hotel.

The Wedgwood Hotel, 1-3 Claremont, was the one-time home of the composer Frederick Delius, who was born across the road at 6 Claremont. He was one of 12 children, his father, Julius having migrated to Bradford from Germany in 1850. After studying music at Leipzig, Delius made his home at Grez-sur-Loing in France, where he remained until his death in June 1934. Bradford made the composer a Freeman of the City in 1932, yet that same year the Council decided to pass up the opportunity to buy Claremont, so robbing future admirers of a memorial and the city of a tourist attraction. This photograph dates from April 1952.

February 1963 and demolition is just a matter of days away for these houses in Richmond Road to make way for the construction of Bradford Institute of Technology. *Bradford Institute of Technology Photographic Studio.*

*Left*: The new Institute of Technology rises above Richmond Road in February 1963. *Bradford Institute of Technology Photographic Studio.*

*Below*: Chesham Street also fell victim to the bulldozers in February 1963. *Bradford Institute of Technology Photographic Studio.*

23501. Bradford, New Connexion Church.

The Vicarage, Great Horton Road, was demolished in 1962 for Bradford Institute of Technology.

Playing instruments akin to modern traffic cones, this band brings a few smiles to the faces of the spectators at the rain-soaked 1907 Great Horton Carnival.

*Opposite page (top):* Ashfield, off Great Horton Road, demolished in 1963, to make way for the Institute of Technology, which became Bradford University in 1966. *Bradford Institute of Technology Photographic Studio.*

*Opposite page (bottom):* The New Connection Chapel, Great Horton Road.

*Top*: A local band leads the parade, followed by the indomitable ladies of the Great Horton Co-operative Women's Guild during the Great Horton Children's Gala of 1911.

*Left*: The 1911 Great Horton Children's Gala gets under way.

*Below*: Low House and brewery were once owned by Joseph Hirst.

Queenbury's triangular station was completed in January 1890, having cost £9,905 to build, whilst the road from the station to the town was completed in 1891 at a cost of £4,641 and replacing an unlit cart track that was a bone of contention, not only with the locals but with the owners of Black Dyke Mills. Fosters had been the principal supporters of the first railway through Queensbury, the Bradford & Thornton Railway, which was built by the Great Northern Railway, a temporary station being opened in April 1879 near the East junction. It was fear of the Midland Railway encroaching on the area that the directors of the Great Northern proposed to build a line from Queensbury to an end-on junction with the Halifax and Ovendon Railway at Holmfield, the contract being awarded to Benton & Woodiwiss for £188,000.

Rail Correspondence and Travel Society rail-tour over the defunct Queensbury lines in September 1964. Passenger services on the Halifax, Bradford-Keighley service via Queensbury had been withdrawn on 23 May 1955, from a number of stations including Great Horton, Clayton Holmfield, Thornton and Cullingworth. The existing facilities for parcels and freight traffic were retained at Great Horton, Holmfield, Thornton, Cullingworth and Ingrow East, whilst Clayton, Queensbury, Denholme and Wilsden were converted into unstaffed freight sidings. Ovenden was closed completely. The last loaded freight train to call at Cullingworth left Thornton on 8 November 1963. *Real Photographs Ltd*

A Bradford tram wends its way down Allerton Road at the turn of the century, untroubled by other traffic.

The people of Allerton built this bonfire to celebrate the Coronation of King Edward VII.

Mostly young Allerton residents pose proudly before the bonfire which marked the 1902 Coronation.

Wallace Holroyd's shop at Queensbury in the 1930s. *Bradford Heritage Recording Unit.*

*Above*: Queensbury from the air in 1922 with Foster's Black Dyke Mills dominating the townscape. Power looms were introduced at Black Dyke in 1836 and the following year the mill began production of alpaca with cotton warps, following the trend set by Titus Salt. *Below*: The junction of Thornton Road and Tyrrel Street in August 1961.

*Above*: C.& J.Clayton, bobbin manufacturers, Boxtree Mills, Thornton Road.

*Left*: Drinking trough for animals on City Road. At one time there would not only be horses looking for a drink but many other beasts too, for the normal method of taking animals to market was on the hoof. Many of these troughs were paid for by animal welfare societies and one or two were built at the termini on horse-drawn tram routes. *Wade Hustwick.*

*Opposite page (top):* Thornton Road looking towards the junction with Listerhills Road and Lower Gratton Road. Just beyond the hoarding for Gold Leaf was Edith's Transport Cafe and the Black Swan (Melbourne Ales), August 1961.

*Opposite page (bottom):* Thornton Road Gasworks is the central feature of this picture taken from an altitude of 750ft (228 metres) in 1928. Bradford Gas Light Co was formed in 1821, the first streets being lit by gas in 1823. In 1871 the company was bought out by the Corporation for £100,000.

The Leaventhorpe Inn, otherwise 1344 Thornton Road, in July 1964. Just out of picture, on the extreme left, is St James' Church, Thornton. *Mabel Bruce.*

St James's School, Thornton, class of 1898.

*Left*: The Bull's Head Inn, Market Street, Thornton, November 1929. The building in the background is the Black Horse Hotel.

Although a Bill was placed before Parliament in 1871, work on the Great Northern's Bradford & Thornton Railway did not begin until 1874, when the £274,000 tender from contractors Benton & Woodiwiss was accepted. Work was slow. Despite being less than six miles in length, the line was a civil engineering nightmare with steep gradients, deep cuttings, high embankments and no less than four tunnels as well as the 20-arch span Thornton Viaduct. Passenger trains commenced in October 1878, a goods service having started some months earlier.

Thornton Market Street.

The Baptist Chapel in Clayton Lane, pictured *c.*1900. This 1891 building replaced the one built in 1830.

The Baptist Sunday School in Clayton Lane, pictured *c.*1900.

Pony and trap outside the Old Dolphin Inn, Clayton Heights, *c.*1900.

The North Brierley Union Workhouse at Clayton, *c.*1900.

The old workhouse at Billy Lane, Clayton Heights, *c.*1900.

*Left:* The former offices of the Bradford Coffee Tavern Company, at the corner of Westgate and Kirkgate, were occupied by Novello & Company when Wade Hustwick took this photograph. The Bradford Coffee Tavern Company was formed in 1878 to 'provide the working-classes alternatives to licenced premises' and had over 20 outlets by the early 1880s. However, the company was wound up in 1903.

*Above:* The Infirmary on White Abbey Road, just up from Westgate, opened in the 1840s, the first use of chloroform as an anaesthetic occurring in 1850 when the entire nursing staff consisted of only four untrained women 'one or more of whom frequently had to be carried to bed in a condition of drunkeness'.

*Opposite (bottom)* The Infirmary was enlarged in 1864, with the addition of a third floor to the original building, and a dispensary was completed several years later, followed in

1885 by a new wing on the Lumb Lane end. However, in 1909 a site for a new Infirmary was surveyed at Field House and was purchased the following year, the first building to be erected being a nurses' hostel in 1920. The new Infirmary had to be built with the help of public subscription, the estimate in 1927 being £500,000 (a battleship then cost around £3 million). The foundation stone of the first patients' block was laid in 1929 and opened to paying patients (remember, this was pre-National Health days) the following year.

Amos Brearley and Mr Wilks were never landlords of this Woolpack in Whetley Hill. Photographed in 1962, the interesting feature is the National Fire Service (NFS) information sign just above the street name-plate. This sign might well have been a throw-back to World War Two, when emergency water supplies were indicated in such a manner in the event of the mains being knocked out by enemy bombing. *Mabel Bruce.*

These two photographs by Mabel Bruce are of the nineteenth-century housing in the Whetley Hill district. In the bottom picture the large building under construction is the Institute of Technology. Note that even in 1962, the streets were still lit by gaslamps.

These two lorries hold a unique place in the history of child welfare in Bradford, for they were used to deliver dinners on the first regular school meals service in the country. It is thanks to the pioneering work of Margaret McMillan, Dr James Kerr and Dr Ralph Crowley that the health and welfare of Bradford's poor children improved. The McMillan sisters arrived in Bradford in 1893 to work for the fledgling Independent Labour Party, but Margaret, who remained in Bradford, was so appalled by the plight of many of the town's children that she resolved to do something about it. Despite having no formal teacher-training or a knowledge of school management, she was elected to the School Board in 1894. She found a staunch ally in Dr James Kerr, School Medical Officer, and between them they were responsible, either wholly or partially, for some notable firsts.

The Bradford 'unemployed' Camp existed for a short while in 1906, on land adjoining Whetley Mills, Girlington. The men seized the land, declaring that they were going to grow vegetables on it, but the idea soon fizzled out. Back in 1837, a trade depression left at least 700 Bradford families with earnings of less than 2s 0d (10p) per head per week.

Digging for Victory? The city's first employment exchange opened in 1910, followed two years later by one for juveniles. During the 1921 slump there were 60,120 unemployed in Bradford, comprising 28,716 men, 26,980 women and 4,524 juveniles.

Picton Street flats, May 1962.

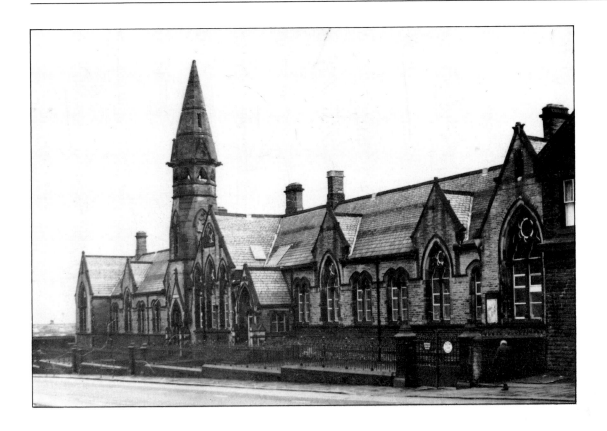

Lilycroft Board School opened in May 1874, the second Board school to be opened in Bradford. In the 1960s and early 1970s, thousands of schools underwent extensive modernization and Lilycroft was no exception. A library was added by constructing a second-floor above the main school room and the hall was equipped to double as a gymnasium. New lighting, floors and plumbing were also included in the programme.

The added library
at Lilycroft Board
School.

Girlington Concertina Band, *c.*1913. One can guess which player had pawned his instrument the day this picture was taken. The man in the centre of the front row is the only one sporting a badge on his cap and it appears to be that of The Green Howards (Alexandra, Princess of Wales's Own Yorkshire Regiment).

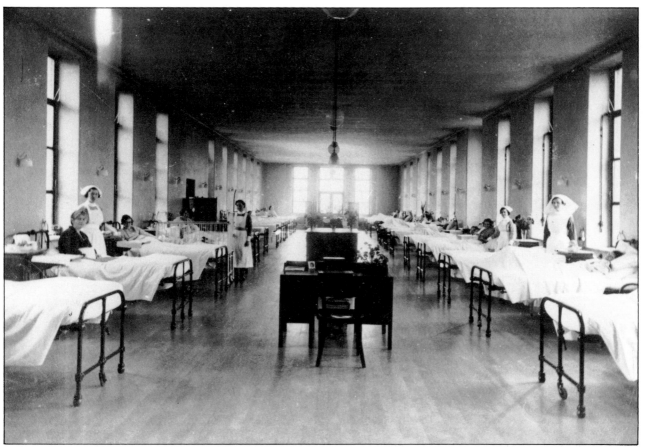

Ward 9 of Bradford Royal Infirmary, Duckworth Lane, in 1938. *Bradford Heritage Recording Unit.*

High Park Farm, Heaton, was a Bradford municipal milk depot and this picture, dating from 1922, shows the sterilising of churns and bottle-washing plant.

*Opposite (top)*: The Yorkshire United Independent College, Emm Lane, Heaton.

*Opposite (bottom)*: Nursemaid and pram, *c.*1890.

*Left*: An outing to Chellow Dene, Heaton, *c.*1900.

The picture that never was. The two boilers were delivered on separate days to Busbys (Bradford) Ltd, Manningham Lane, but by a piece of photographic skullduggery it has been made to look as though they arrived together. In the mid-1930s, Busbys embarked on an expansion programme, increasing their retail sales area to at least 125,000 sq ft. *Bradford Heritage Recording Unit.*

*Opposite page (top)*: Bradford's second Theatre Royal was in Manningham Lane and opened in 1864 as The Royal Alexandra Theatre. In 1867 the original Theatre Royal in Duke Street was demolished and the change in name took place. It became a cinema in 1921.

*Opposite page (bottom)*: When this photograph was taken in 1972, the former Marlboro' Cinema, Carlisle Road, Manningham, was already in its fourth year as the Liberty Cinema showing Asian films. The Marlboro' had opened in November 1921 but closed to adult film-goers on 10 October 1962, the last film show for the Star Junior's Club taking place three days later. For several years the building was used as a bingo club but the sessions were transferred to the Elite, Toller Lane, in 1968.

*Below:* A parade of fire appliances passes the corner of Snowdon Street and Manningham Lane, *c.*1908-09. Historically significant is the motor fire pump, as not only was this Bradford's first motorised engine, it was also the first one built by Dennis. It was equipped with a single-stage centrifugal pump supplied by Gwynne Cars Ltd and powered by a White & Popple engine. It ran on solid tyres.

*Right:* The old library interior, Carlisle Road, Manningham.

This snowscape forms the subject of a private Christmas postcard sent by Mr and Mrs C.H.Wood. Mr Wood, an excellent photographer, went on to establish a very successful commercial photography business in Bradford. The card is thought to date from immediately before World War One.

*Right* The leather department at Manningham Mills, *c.*1919. *Bradford Heritage Recording Unit.*

*Opposite page (top):* Manningham Mills with its distinctive chimney, photographed during the 1920s. The original Manningham Mill was opened in 1838 under the name of J.C. & S.Lister and in 1843 switched to machine woolcombing of Botany product following successful experiments carried out by S.C.Lister and G.E.Donisthorpe. The mill was destroyed by fire in 1871 but quickly rebuilt. *N.S.Roberts.*

*Opposite page (bottom):* The Bradford Exhibition was opened at Lister Park on 4 May 1904 by the Prince and Princess of Wales, to celebrate the completion of Cartwright Hall. When the exhibition finally closed the following November, around 2.5 million people had visited the site.

*Below:* Finishing fabrics. Embossing pile fabrics at Manningham Mills, *c.*1919. *Bradford Heritage Recording Unit.*

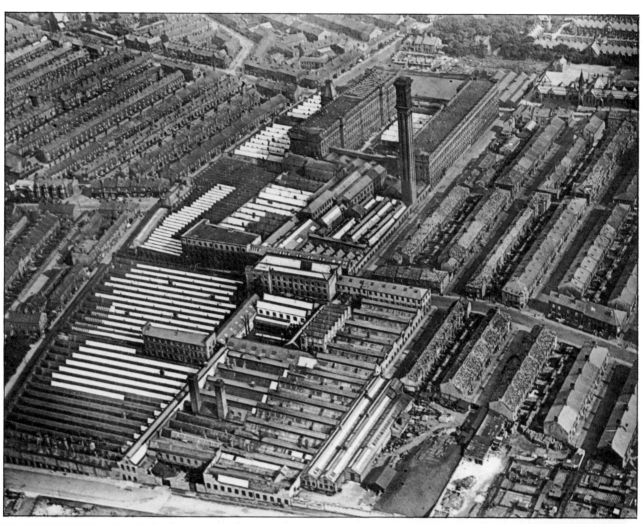

*Lister Park in 1924 N.S.Roberts.*

*Above*: Amongst the attractions at the Bradford Exhibition were this waterchute, a switchback ride, the crystal maze, an industrial hall, concert hall and a Somali village.

*Below*: The vast majority of visitors to the exhibition would have found the Somali village no more than an interesting insight into another culture, whilst old soldiers would no doubt have reminisced about their experience in the nearby Sudan in the 1880s and 1890s. But in the Victorian/ Edwardian period there was a popular view of evolution that the different races represented different stages of human development with Africans at the bottom, Asians in the middle and white Europeans at the top. Two years after the Bradford Exhibition, an African pygmy was exhibited in the same cage as a chimpanzee at the Bronx Zoo. It caused an uproar, not because it degraded both man and chimpanzee but because it promoted the idea that the apes and humans were related.

Somali villagers perform one of their native dances.

Cartwright Hall shortly after completion in 1904.

Lister Park in September 1965. *Aerofilms Ltd.*

The finishing touches are put to an exhibition of war photographs at Cartwright Hall. If this is the same exhibition that was mounted in Leeds, then the photographs had all been coloured-in. *Imperial War Museum.*

*Previous page*: Car No.4 of Bradford Tramways at the Lister Park terminus. This vehicle was one of six supplied in 1882 by the Ashbury Carriage and Wagon Company and carried 18 passengers inside and 20 on the top deck. Only two routes were operated with horse-drawn trams — North Park Road and Frizinghall. By 1886 most, if not all, of the horse trams had been fitted with three-quarter length covers to the top deck.

Tram locomotive No.24 and double-decker passenger trailer No.28 at Frizinghall in 1889. The locomotive was one of 29 built for Bradford Tramways by E.Green & Sons, others were supplied by Kitson & Company, William Wilkinson & Company and Beyer Peacock & Company. The trailer was ordered from G.F.Milnes & Company, who sub-contracted the work to Ashbury Carriage and Wagon Company. The route to Frizinghall was extended to Shipley in 1893, although Bradford was already showing an interest in electric traction. On 1 February 1902, the Corporation bought out the Bradford Tramways and Omnibus Company for £30,000 and the construction of overhead wiring along the steam routes got underway, the last route to be converted to electric traction being Peel Park to Undercliffe on 28 June. All the steam locomotives were sold and most of the trailers broken up, although one or two were converted into works vehicles.

*Above*: A tram stands at the entrance to Lister Park.

*Opposite page (top)*: Bradford's great man of letters, J.B.Priestley, takes a break during the filming of *The Lost City* for BBC TV at Frizinghall.

*Opposite page (bottom)*: Bradford Arts Club supper at Hanover Square in 1938. Standing (left to right): Mr Taylor, E.M.Cox, F.Bradshaw, unknown, J.H.Trout, J.Garforth, W.B.Tapp, Cottam and Fred Stead. Seated: C.H.Wood, E.M.Leighton, P.Monkman, J.B.Priestley, R.H.Facey, J.Brown and Alex Keighley.

Tordoff & Son were based in Bradford but maintained a London office at 21 Mincing Lane.

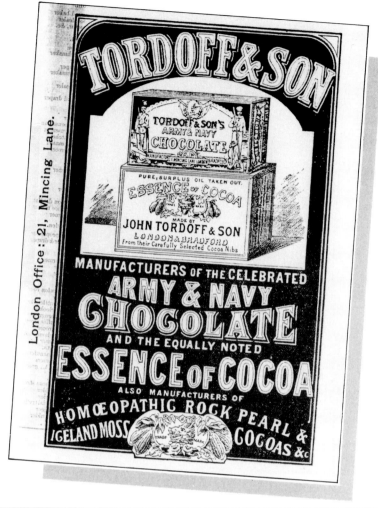

Members of the 6th Battalion, Prince of Wales's Own West Yorkshire Regiment are mobilized in August 1914. They saw action in several battles including Ypres and Passchendaele and were later part of the occupation force in Germany.

*Left*: The Western Front, *c*.1916. In September 1914, the 2/6th Battalion, West Yorkshire Regiment was raised at Belle Vue Barracks as a reserve unit for the original 6th Battalion. They later fought at Cambrai. On 14 May 1922, the battalion's colours were laid up for safe keeping in the Cathedral. A unique record held by the original 6th Battalion is that it was the first Territorial Army unit to report ready for active duty in World War One.

*Below*: Troops march along Tong Street, possibly a detachment of one of the Pals Battalions. The idea behind the raising of the Pals Battalions was that men from a particular area of a town or from the same occupation could enlist, train and fight together; alas, no thought was given to the fact that they might die together. The 1st Bradford Pals (16th West Yorkshire) Battalion was soon joined by a second battalion (18th West Yorkshire). At a poignant ceremony in July 1979, a plaque in memory of the battalions was unveiled in Bradford Cathedral by the Lord Mayor, Councillor John Senior. The standard of the Pals Association was presented to the Provost, the Very Reverend Brandon Jackson, for laying up.

Signals platoon, Bradford Pals.

30 August 1940. HRH The Princess Royal visited the 50th Battalion, West Yorkshire Regiment at Wetherby Racecourse. This battalion's recruits were predominantly from Leeds and Bradford and when these pictures were taken they had been in uniform for between eight and ten weeks. The 50th was one of a number of battalions raised in the months following Dunkirk, primarily for home defence duties. But following the setbacks in the Far East, Greece and Crete, many were renumbered and eventually fought overseas, whilst others were converted into training units. In the above picture, the Princess Royal inspects a guard of honour provided by 'C' Company. *Imperial War Museum.*

'A' Company get to grips with a couple of Bren guns. Developed from a Czech design, it was one of the best infantry weapons of the Second World War. Very accurate, its only drawback being the magazine which held only 30 rounds of ammunition. *Imperial War Museum.*

Valley Parade, the home of Bradford City FC. The origins of the football club go back to Manningham, a rugby side who played on a ground in Carlisle Road. After moving to Valley Parade, the club took up playing soccer and under the name Bradford City were elected to the Second Division of the Football League in 1903. Promoted to the First Division in 1908, three years later they won the FA Cup after beating Newcastle United in a replay. The biggest attendance at Valley Parade was 37,059 for a Third Division North game against local rivals, Bradford Park Avenue, in September 1927. *Aerofilms Ltd.*

The Valley Road district in 1925.

View up Otley Road from North Wing in December 1964.

The Tennyson Picture House, Otley Road, opened its doors to cinemagoers on Monday 15 October 1923 with *Moran of the Mary Letty* starring Rudolf Valentino. The supporting picture was the exclusive showing of *The Japanese Earthquake*, an early documentary about the destruction wreaked on Tokyo earlier in the year when at least 300,000 people were killed in the initial 'quake. Some 800,000 perished by tidal waves and thousands more killed by cholera and other diseases. *N.Stow, courtesy of Mrs Mary Stow.*

Courtyard on the east side of Otley Road, August 1960. *Mabel Bruce.*

*Above and opposite:* All the fun of the fair at Peel Park in 1908 featured one of the first helter-skelter rides in Britain. Other rides included steam roundabouts — one of which was Waddington's Racing Horses — swingboats and side-shows. Peel Park had been bought from its owners in 1850 for use as a public park under the control of trustees, the first gala taking place in 1853. The park passed into local authority control in 1863.

The star of the 1908 gala was the balloon. The first aeroplane to fly over Bradford was still a year away and that would manage to travel only 300 yards at the heady height of 15ft.

Police officers on parade at Peel Park. Bradford Borough Police came into existence on 1 January 1848, although there had been paid constables since 1831. Peel Park was also used for reviews of volunteer units of the army including the Yeomanary and Militia. *Bradford Heritage Recording Unit.*

Undercliffe School in 1922 when the teacher of the girls' class was Miss Kershaw and the headmistress was Mrs Heaton. Boys and girls were taught in separate classes, and had separate assemblies and playgrounds.

Idle in 1925. *N.S.Roberts.*

A general view of the
town from Cliff
Quarry in the Bolton
Road area, *c*.1872.

The Green, Idle, in 1973 still had the air of a village.

The 5,000th B250 tractor is turned out by International Harvesters at their plant in the former Jowett car factory, Idle.

Greenside Mill, Idle in 1922. *N.S.Roberts.*

*Opposite (top):* This photograph is used to show one of the many processes involved in the worsted industry. There was a time when wool sorting was potentially lethal. In the early 1860s, Mohair was introduced into Bradford and although all went well at first, isolated cases of anthrax in workers engaged in wool sorting began to be reported. In 1878 the first fatality occurred from anthrax that could be positively linked to Mohair. Further deaths occurred in 1879, and in 1880 a coroner's jury requested that regulations for the handling of Mohair, Cape Hair and all hair and wools from Persia (Iran) and the East be introduced. By 1884 a code governing wool sorting was in use and in 1895 the Home Office began to take an interest in the fight to prevent the disease. The local Chamber of Commerce and the Trades Council thrashed out a new code adopted by all firms involved in handling dangerous wools, but even so outbreaks of the disease continued. In 1910 there were 51 cases throughout

Yorkshire, of which nine were fatal. It was to be the mid-1930s before anthrax was effectively brought under control, largely due to the efforts of Dr F.W.Eurich of Bradford.

*Opposite (bottom):* The Bradford Moor housing scheme takes shape in 1925. In 1917, the Local Government Board appointed a committee chaired by Sir John Tudor Walters to come up with improved housing for the working classes. Sir John's committee laid down minimum standards of three bedrooms, kitchen, bath, parlour, electric lighting and gas or electric for cooking, as well as a maximum density of 12 houses per acre. Legislation also required these houses to be built away from old crowded districts, a move that gave us the housing estate. The main drawback of the new estates was that the warmth, neighbourliness and structure of the old communities was lacking.

*Above:* Tramcar No.116 trundles along an otherwise traffic-free Leeds Road on the through service to Leeds. The Leeds and Bradford tramways operated on different gauges and a through service could not be introduced until the problem was solved with the development of an adjustable truck. By 1909, 21 trams had been fitted with the truck and were in service. Also in the photograph is an advertisement for Hibbert's Pictures. Henry Hibbert's interest in movies had started as a hobby and most of his films were of his worldwide travels. For his work he was awarded a Fellowship of the Royal Geographical Society. Films were also shown in Eastbrook Hall, where in 1913 the Reverend Gilbert Muir showed movies and lantern slides, again of an educational nature.

Despite one of two minor French incursions, the Channel Islands had been British since the Norman Conquest, but when France was overrun in 1940, Jersey, Guernsey, Alderney and Sark were obvious targets for invasion by the Germans. During the last week of June the islands witnessed their own 'Dunkirk' as every available vessel was pressed into service for the hazardous 24-hour crossing to Weymouth. In all 25,000 people were evacuated before the Germans arrived. Bradford's Eastbrook Hall was one of the reception centres for these evacuees.

*Bottom right*: Refugees are kitted out with shoes and spare clothing as many had had to leave with few, if any, personal possessions. 24 June 1940. *Imperial War Museum.*

*Above (left)*: Nurses of the Bradford Civil Nursing Reserve look after the very young. 24 June 1940. *Imperial War Museum.*

*Above (right)*: A member of the WVS gets on with the paperwork. 24 June 1940. *Imperial War Museum.*

*Opposite (top)*: The sandwich-board men comment. *Charles Pratt.*

*Opposite (bottom)*: The congregation of Eastbrook Hall poses for the camera in this pre-World War One photograph. *Charles Pratt.*

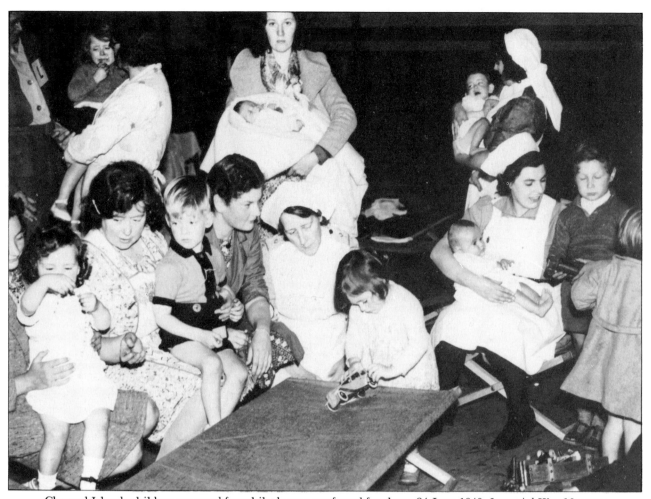

Channel Islands children are cared for whilst homes are found for them. 24 June 1940. *Imperial War Museum.*

The old Eastbrook Chapel stood on the corner of Leeds Road and Chapel Street and was replaced in the early 1900s by Eastbrook Hall.

# HOLDSWORTH & SONS

MANUFACTURERS OF

## BOILERS OF ALL DESCRIPTIONS

Telephone No. 446.

Telegraphic Address:
"Steam, Bradford."

—— CROFT BOILER WORKS, ——
LAUREL STREET, LEEDS ROAD, BRADFORD.

*Below:* The Cash-
mere Mills, Leeds
Road, from an aerial
picture of 1924.
*N.S.Roberts.*

The tram and 'bus depot at Thornbury, seen from the air in 1928. The adjoining workshops built many of Bradford's trams and some of the early trolly buses. In the far distance is the Dick Lane foundry of English Electric. *N.S.Roberts.*

Tramcar decorated for the Coronation of King George V in 1911.

Car No.104 decked out for its role as Bradford's last tram before it went on to a subsequent career as the score-board at Odsal Stadium. In 1958 the tram was lovingly restored to working order by a dedicated band of enthusiasts and in March 1975 she was moved to the Industrial Museum at Moorside Mills.

The English Electric works at Dick Lane in 1928. *N.S.Roberts.*

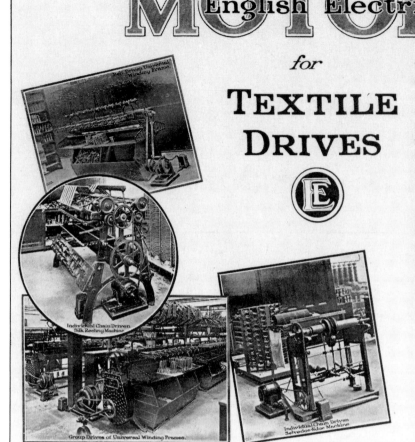

# "English Electric" MOTORS

## for TEXTILE DRIVES

The name **"English Electric"** is your **Greatest Guarantee** of Quality and Service. Hundreds of thousands of Motors built in the Bradford Works of The English Electric Company and supplied some **ten-fifteen-twenty** and more **years** ago continue to give **uninterrupted service.** Such unassailable evidence is a surety to the buyer of lasting performance without troublesome restrictions or conditions at time of purchase. Nowhere is a fuller advisory service, both technical and practical, available to buyers than in the organisation of The English Electric Company. The illustrations show "English Electric" Motor drives applied to the silk and artificial silk industries. Electric Driving gives Economy, Convenience, and Simplicity to an extent which no alternative kind of power can offer.

## MOTORS FOR A.C. AND D.C.

The first re-armament orders were placed with the Phoenix Works in June 1938, for sound locators for use with searchlights. More orders followed including fire directors for warships
In 1938, Rushton Mills were bought and turned into machine shops. Many other armament orders followed.

These pictures (*left and opposite page*) are of the visit by Prime Minister Winston Churchill to the Phoenix Works site of English Electric in December 1942. On his whistle-stop tour of Yorkshire and the North East, Churchill was accompanied by his wife and by the Rt Hon Ernest Bevin and Sir Archibald Sinclair. Churchill was shown around the Phoenix Works by (later Sir) George Nelson. *Imperial War Museum.*

The east side of Laisterdyke looking south to north. The Old Queen's Hall cinema closed in June 1957. The 500-seater cinema had opened in October 1911 under the management of Mr Louis Prosser for Jury's Imperial Pictures, in what was the former St Paul's Church building dating from 1857. The building has since been demolished. *Mabel Bruce.*

*Below*: Laisterdyke, east side, looking north to south towards Sticker Lane in March 1961. *Mabel Bruce.*

*Above:* Trolley bus No.240, one of a pair built by Hurst Nelson for Britain's first trackless tram system. By 1920 a further 21 trolley buses were in service including No.521, the first double-decker. The first route was Laisterdyke to Dudley Hill. Not only did Bradford operate Britain's first trolley bus system, it also operated the last. Despite running at a profit the system closed in March 1972.

*Left*: Bradford aerodrome in 1924 was a field at Quarry Gap, Laisterdyke. Whether the crowd had turned out to watch N.S.Roberts fly his photomission or if there was something else in the air, we shall probably never know.

Trolley bus and camera fascinate the locals. This view is taken in Laisterdyke, on the Dudley Hill side of the traffic lights. It is a posed view, probably to show the flexibility of the trolley bus in its ability, unlike the tramcar, to overtake other traffic.

*Right*: The first temperance society in England was formed in Bradford in 1830 and followed in 1843 by the Long Pledge Teetotal Association. In 1878, the Bradford Coffee Tavern Company was established but went out of business in 1903. As can be seen, at least one former coffee tavern fell into the hands of the 'enemy'. Sticker Lane, January 1961. *Mabel Bruce.*

*Below*: The east side of Sticker Lane showing Marsden Fold, February 1961. *Mabel Bruce.*

*Opposite page (top)*: The Church of the First Martyrs at Cutler Heights in 1972. Bradford's first Roman Catholic church since the Reformation, St Mary's, was consecrated in 1825, prior to which those wishing to hear a mass had had to travel to Leeds, where a church had been opened in 1794. Between 1535 and 1753, if there were practising Roman Catholics in Bradford, then they succeeded in maintaining their faith in absolute secrecy throughout a period that witnessed the very worst excesses of religious intolerence. During the early years of the nineteenth century, an influx of Irish immigrant cloth workers helped swell the ranks of the Catholic community and by 1822, Bradford had a resident priest. A mass was celebrated in the Roebuck Inn but the landlady was warned that her licence was in jeopardy so a room was hired in Toad Lane, which was on the site of the present City Hall, and this remained in use until St Mary's was ready. Bradford's second Catholic Church, St Patrick's, was consecrated in 1853.

*Opposite page (bottom)*: The junction of Cutler Heights Lane, Mullcott Road and Sticker Lane in 1962. In the centre background can be seen the gates of Greenfield Greyhound Stadium which opened in 1927. The city's second dog track opened at Legrams Lane in 1932. Both closed in the mid-1960s. Greyhound racing was a phenomenon of the 1920s, a mechanical hare first being used in Manchester in 1926. By 1929, betting totalled £8 million a year compared with £3 million on newspaper football competitions (forerunners of the pools). The National Greyhound Racing Association controlled the sport and by 1932 they operated 23 tracks with 4,000 days of racing and attendances of 20 million. The tote first appeared on an English track in 1934 with the passing of the Betting and Lotteries Act, although subject to a limit of 104 days racing on each course.

*Above:* Bowling Back Lane was Bradford's first Board school to open following the implementation of the 1870 Education Act. By 1874, eight Board schools were operating and others were either under construction or projected. As a stop-gap, Sunday schools were rented.

*Right:* Bowling Iron Works, *c.*1861. The company was founded in 1788 as an offshoot of the Fall Ings Works, Wakefield, for the manufacture of a wide range of iron products. But even though the firm used the very latest equipment and produced the very best wrought-iron, like Low Moor it was to pay the price for failing to take steel-making seriously and went out of business.

*Above:* Bowling Iron Works in 1894. During the Napoleonic Wars, Bowling's iron guns had equipped warships and foot and horse artillery, seeing action at Trafalgar and Waterloo.

During World War One, the number of women in employment rose from just under 6 million to 7.3 million, the bulk of the jobs being in the munitions industry. At the same time, the number of women in domestic service fell by 400,000. Within a year of the Armistice, 750,000 women had been dismissed and it was back to the same old jobs, domestic service, textiles, clothing, shop assistants with a minority working in offices or as teachers.

*Left (upper):* Making light work of a heavy load at J.T.Hardaker, Bowling, using a U-framed jack truck for lifting weights from 3cwts to 5cwts. *Imperial War Museum.*

*Left (lower):* Ancestor of the fork-lift truck in use at J.T.Hardaker was the hand-operated elevator truck, whilst above is the jack truck designed to lift a maximum of 10cwt. *Imperial War Museum.*

*Above:* Wakefield Road opposite Bowling Road. The large building is the Adolphus Street Goods Depot, the original Great Northen Railway Station until passenger traffic was transferred to Exchange Station.

*Below:* The approach to Adolphus Street Station. August 1963. *F.D.Smith.*

*Above:* The Wakefield Road end of Hall Lane in 1960.

*Below*: Not an army camp but prefabricated housing at Hall Lane. Thousands of prefabs were erected nationwide in an effort to ease the chronic housing shortage at the end of World War Two. The concept of prefab housing was that they would be redundant within a few years, having been superseded by more permanent accommodation. The Hall Lane estate lasted until 1960, although in some parts of the country prefabs were still in use in the 1990s. An interesting feature of the Hall Lane estate was the use of obsolete Anderson air-raid shelters as garden sheds. *N.Stow, courtesy of Mrs Mary Stow.*

Usher Street Infants School in 1914. It was at Usher Street that the first school medical in the country was held in about 1899.

Wakefield Road Baths in 1905.

The late 1960s early 1970s saw areas flattened to allow road widening schemes to proceed. This is the A650 Wakefield Road on a slushy day in January 1970.

Foundry Lane off Wakefield Road was the entrance to Bowling bus depot. Built by the Corporation in 1905 to house tramcars, it was converted for use by buses in the late 1930s, although trams were stored there awaiting disposal. During World War Two the depot was used by the ARP services, reverting to Corporation control on the cessation of hostilities. The depot closed in 1978.

Opened in 1913, the Coventry Cinema was housed in a former Bradford Coffee Tavern Company building. Housing a cosy 400 customers, the Coventry was altered in 1930 by the addition of a mock-Tudor frontage. The cinema closed its doors on Saturday, 12 December 1959, and was bulldozed for the widening of Wakefield Road.

Wakefield Road looking towards the city from Dudley Hill in 1960.

The crossroad at Dudley Hill in 1960, looking towards the city with its array of trolley bus overhead wires.

Dudley Hill looking towards the city in 1960.

The Tudor Cafe, Dudley Hill, on the south side of Tong Street in March 1961. *Mabel Bruce.*

Dudley Hill Socialist Club.

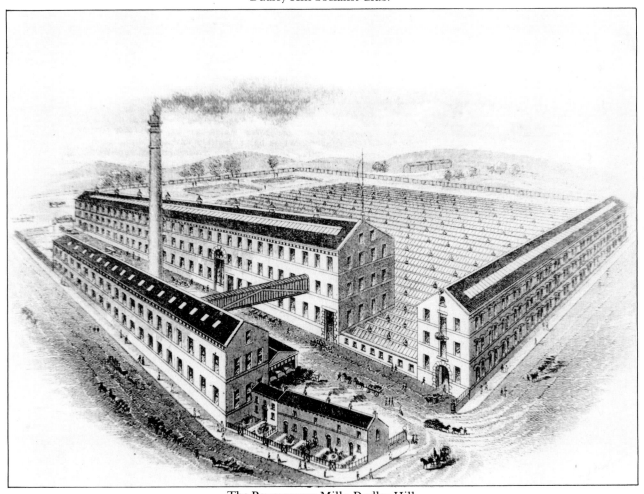

The Perseverance Mills, Dudley Hill.

Tong Street, Dudley Hill in 1960.

This picture and the one shown at top of the next page are separated by 11 years, the reference points being the mill building and the Picture Palace. This cinema opened in December 1912 and was the first in the city to be equipped with oil-fired central heating. The last double feature to be shown was *Thunderbirds Are Go*, a feature-length film based on Gerry Anderson's series for ABC TV and *Beauty and the Beast* starring Joyce Taylor. *Mabel Bruce*.

By 1971, the Picture Palace had been a bingo hall for about four years.

Dudley Hill from the air in 1924. *N.S.Roberts.*

A Whitsun treat for East Bowling Socialist Sunday School.

The Old Red Ginn, Bowling Old Lane, was opened before 1735 and catered to the needs of local imbibers until it fell victim to a clearance scheme and was demolished. Before World War One it was the HQ of Bradford Northern RLFC, who no doubt indulged in some serious training in the four-ale bar. *Wade Hustwick*.

Taken for the West Bowling Survey was this photograph looking up Newton Street from the corner of Wootton Street. *N.Stow, courtesy of Mrs Mary Stow.*

The top side of Wootton Street looking towards Coates Terrace with Newton Street on the left. *N.Stow, courtesy of Mrs Mary Stow.*

The ubiquitous charabanc. Trips in these machines were extremely popular in the 1910s and 1920s.

Willie Binns with Bradford's earliest motor-taxi.

In 1907, Bradford Corporation had the unique distinction of being the only local authority in the country to operate a light railway. The Nidd Valley Light Railway was an integral part of a massive water supply scheme for the city which included the construction of new reservoirs at Angram and Scar House. *Above:*Nidd Valley Railway locomotive department depot in 1928. On the shed are the locomotive *Blythe* and the former Great Western steam railcar.

The locomotive *Milner* crossing the new rail-road bridge at Lofthouse in 1928.

Four-engined goods train highballs up the gradient near Wath in 1928.

The service reservoir at Horton Bank. *C.H.Wood for Bradford Waterworks.*

Southwaite compensation reservoir. Similar installations were built at Grimwith, Silsden, Doe Park, Hewenden, Leeming and Leeshaw. *C.H.Wood for Bradford Waterworks.*

Chellow Heights filtration plant at the end of the 32-mile long supply line from the Nidd Valley, where water is filtered to remove discolouration due to the peaty nature of the soil at the foot of Great Whernside. *C.H.Wood for Bradford Waterworks.*

Scar House reservoir cost £2.2 million to build and has a capacity of 2,200 million gallons, the smallest reservoir in the system being Hewenden with its 93 million gallons. Scar was built to provide the area with 13.3 million gallons per day. *C.H.Wood for Bradford Waterworks.*

Gilstead filtration plant. *C.H.Wood for Bradford Waterworks.*

The Tyrls in November 1971. On the extreme left is the HQ of the Provincial Building Society whilst the building immediately behind the double-decker 'bus is Britannia House, built in the early 1930s.

*Overleaf:* Tram route 7 ran to Thornton and this picture may have been taken before Thornton Road was widened between the wars.

# Further Reading

*Bradford* Joseph Fieldhouse, (Bradford Libraries) 1878.
*Bradford* David James (Ryburn Publishing) 1990.
*Pen and Pencil Sketches of Old Bradford 1889* William Scruton. (Reprinted by Amethyst Press) 1990.
*Centenary Book of Bradford 1847-1947* (Yorkshire Observer) 1947.
*Victorian Bradford* D.C.Wright and J.A.Jowitt (Bradford Libraries) 1982.
*A Geography of Bradford* C.Richardson (University of Bradford) 1976.
*Historical Notes on the Bradford Corporation* William Cudworth (Brear) 1881.
*How a City Grows* Horace Hird (Author) 1966.
*The Victorian Houses of Bradford* George Sheeran (Bradford Libraries) 1990.
*Bradford's Police* George Smith (City of Bradford Police) 1974.
*Bradford Corporation Waterworks: A Centenary Handbook* (Bradford Corporation) 1955.
*Education in Bradford Since 1870* (Bradford Corporation) 1970
*Bradford's Railways Remembered* Alan Whitaker (Dalesman) 1986.
*Bradford City Tramways 1882-1950* D.M.Coates (Wyvern Publications) 1984.
*Transport of Delight: the Bradford Trollybus 1911-1972* J.S.King (National Trollybus Association) 1972.
*Reminiscences of a Bradford Mill Girl* Maggie Newbury (Bradford Libraries) 1980.
*Textile Voices: Mill Life This Century* Bradford Heritage Recording Unit (Bradford Libraries) 1989.
*Destination Bradford: A Century of Immigration* Bradford Heritage Recording Unit (Bradford Libraries) 1987.
*The Bradford Almanack* Edward H.Johnson (Bradford Libraries) 1990.

# SUBSCRIBERS

## Presentation Copy

### 1 The City of Bradford

2 Paul Lawson
3 John Triffitt
4 R J Duckett
5 Mr Frederick Trevor Kellett Jagger
6 A Feather
7 Terry Frost
8 Albert Ollerenshaw
9 Jeffrey Tucker
10 Colin Mellor
11 Cynthia Shepherd
12 Peter Stanley
13 Brian S Crossland
14 Michael Jagger
15 L G Illingworth
16 Paul Hirst
17 David Miller
18 T & E Pearson
19 Irene S Kirk
20 Irene S Kirk
21 Brian Dickinson
22 Kevin Narey
23 John Burns
24 Peter & Valerie Hall
25 Hilton Whitaker
26 Peter Scowcroft
27 George Softley
28 Bob Watson
29 Stephen T Garnham
30 G L Parkinson
31 R M Krahmer
32 Bill Robinson
33 Margaret Jagger
34 Philip Smith
35 David Archer
36 David Ratcliffe
37 Percy Clayburn
38 Percy Clayburn
39 Albert E Bowtell
40 Edna Hirst
41 Philip Rushworth
42 Phillip Priestley
43 Eric Wilson

44 D J Clayton
45 Mr Michael Thwaites
46 Mrs Patricia Watson
47 Anthony Sheard
48 Mr Ian Hudson
49 Keith Farrell
50 Mrs Maureen H Brosco MBE
51 Mr W L Barrett
52 Mrs Margaret Lee
53 Beverley Ann Parkes
54 Mrs Mary Hemingway
55 D M King
56 Malcolm Robertshaw
57 Stella Patricia Keyte
58 Donald A Cunnington
59 George Clarke
60 Keith Clark
61 Kenneth Holmes
62 Doreen Hocks
63 Geoffrey C Burn
64 Geoffrey C Burn
65 Celia M Taylor
66 Joan Grayshon
67 Ann Davies
68 Mr R S Brown
69 Gladys E Broughton
70 Susan Ryland
71 John Pickles
72 Mrs Marjorie Stell
73 Charlotte E Wright
74 Joyce Lawrenson
75 K M Byrne
76 E Broadley
77 Arthur Calvert Wormald
78 Anthony L West
79 Dr Margaret Cole
80 Mrs Doreen Ward
81 Mr W Sutcliffe
82 J G Prentice
83 Roy North
84 Kenneth A Webster
85 James Derek Willis

86 Christopher J Espert
87 Audrey Midgley
88 Donald A Wilson
89 Brian Burrows
90 Kevin Flaherty
91 Jean Craven
92 Terence Rowley
93 Andrew Leith
94 Graham T Reid
95 Mr A W Buxton
96 A Thompson
97 Ronnie Diaczenko
98 Mr F Baxter
99 Joseph Jackson
100 Jack Bates
101 David Poskett
102 Brian Tonks
103 Philip Holmes
104 E Sunderland
105 Sydney Lawrence
106 Joan Goldsbrough
107 William Bywater
108 Anthony Brian Waterworth
109 Noreen L Brooke
110 Alice Foster
111 David Fenton
112 Mary Wallace
113 Mary Wallace
114 Mrs Doreen Myers
115 W G Stephenson
116 Marjorie Ellen Acton
117 Mrs Anne Elsworth
118 John Wilford
119 Betty Wood
120 Peter Baren
121 David Wormald
122 Cyril Hargreaves
123 K Moore
124 Leslie James Collins
125 Raymond Schofield
126 William Hill
127 Mr N G Muff
128 C D Holdsworth

129 S D Holdsworth
130 Simon Peter Emmerson
131 Mr & Mrs Peter D Walker
132 Jack Rhodes
133 Mr C Wharton
134 Raymond Hanson
135 Jean Nichols
136 Robert M Hanson
137 David Bould
138 Maureen Sykes
139 Mr Kenneth Emmerson
140 John Kennedy
141 Robert J R Allan
142 Mr John Stewart Wilson
143 Josephine L Pollard
144 Edna McMahon
145 Thomas Andrew Murray
    Carter

146 Barbara Fortune
147 Betty Roast
148 Derek David Burgess
149 Brian & Norma Shillaker
150 Mrs B Gee
151 Derek Pickles
152 Mrs Joan Stocks
153 Reg Nelson
154 Sheila M Varo
155 Mrs I Burn
156 Harry Bennett
157 Maurice Beaumont
158 Andrew Thornton
159 Mr N Kenney
160 Mr R Gilmour
161 J M Kershaw
162 Nicola Robinson

163 Geoff F Craven
164 Shirley Williamson
165 John Moss
166 George Donald & Joan
    Carter
167 John Joseph McDonald
168 Francis C Naylor
169 Shirley M Naylor
170 B Collett
171 Colin Illingworth
172 William Harrison
173 Joan Honey
174 Kenneth Gawthorpe
175 Clifford Pollard
176 Karen Elizabeth Mundy
177 Kevin Mundy
178 Mrs Audrey Hepworth